HOT TUB
SPACESHIP

*Irradiated Thoughts on God,
Life, and $#*! like that.*

Brian A. Pankratz

 FriesenPress

Suite 300 - 990 Fort St
Victoria, BC, V8V 3K2
Canada

www.friesenpress.com

ISBN
978-1-5255-1731-0 (Hardcover)
978-1-5255-1732-7 (Paperback)
978-1-5255-1733-4 (eBook)

1. BIOGRAPHY & AUTOBIOGRAPHY, PERSONAL MEMOIRS

Distributed to the trade by The Ingram Book Company

Table of Contents

Part Seven
THE MULTIVERSE

Part Eight
THE VOYAGE HOME

For Hudson and Ellie,

These were written for you.

I love you both very much.

I am on the fence about nearly everything I've seen
And I have felt the fire get put out by too much gasoline
And we're all strangers passing through a place and time and an afternoon
Life is but a vision in a window that we're peeking through

A helpless conversation with a man who says he cares a lot
It's a passive confrontation about who might throw a punch or not
We are all transgressors, we're all sinners, we're all astronauts
So if you're beating death then raise your hand but shut up if you're not

-NEEDTOBREATHE

FOREWORD

Brian and I have been friends and fellow writers since creative writing class in grade twelve at Nanaimo District Secondary School. Our teacher, Mr. Rodney Brown, was a tough marker. Was he as tough as my editors today? Perhaps not. But for teens with fragile egos and little experience, Mr. Brown was super tough!

When Brian asked me to provide input on *Hot Tub Spaceship*, the question I asked myself was not, "Will I do it?" but "How Mr. Brown-like should I be?" My answer (I hope) was, "Just Mr. Brown-like enough." I pointed out the bigger areas for potential improvement and left a few smaller areas alone. And through it all, it was a pleasure to spend time with Brian's mind, heart, and soul via these pages.

Hot Tub Spaceship is candid, honest, and a whole lot of fun. Make no mistake: Brian preaches more than just a little (what would you expect from an ex-pastor?), but he avoids coming across as preachy by simultaneously serving up heaping helpings of humor and self-deprecation. He doesn't hide his viewpoint, but he doesn't hide his doubts either. He calls bullshit on others but calls bullshit on himself most of all.

Many new writers struggle to find their voice. While Brian has certainly struggled with all the crap that life threw his way, there is no sign of any struggle with his voice. It feels effortless and natural from the start. Brian's writerly voice is clear, consistent, and compelling—not to mention endearing as all get out. His conversational tone is eminently readable and exceedingly genuine.

This book gave me the opportunity to walk alongside—and see inside—a keen, curious observer of the world and the human condition. Work of this caliber would be an achievement if it had been created during the best of times. This book is even more remarkable given the tumultuous circumstances under which Brian was writing.

But I have saved the highest praise for last, and it is this: Mr. Brown would be proud, Brian. Take a well-deserved bow.

—Troy Wilson, Author,
Perfect Man, The Duck Says, and *Liam Takes a Stand*

HOT TUB
SPACESHIP

Part One

FIRST FLIGHT

Every year another promise is made

A pint of beer raised towards a better day

Let's find a star, a star to call our own

And make a wish,

maybe we can make it home

—EDWIN

WARM BLANKETS

Radiation therapy for my brain tumor began today. The technicians at the cancer clinic strapped my head to a long bench, taped stickers to my eyelids, and placed a warm blanket on my body. All life-changing moments should begin with a warm blanket.

After about five minutes of clicking sounds and zapping lasers that reminded me of the Kraftwerk music I used to listen to in junior high, my first treatment was over. My head hurt, and my eyes felt like shit, but I was happy to be done. The techs returned and undid the five clamps that held my head in position and said, "See you tomorrow morning, Brian."

Easy for them to say. Their eyes don't feel like shit.

I know I responded with a much nicer pleasantry and then left the building. It wasn't long before I was ocularly fine again. My emotional health, however, was another matter. There's nothing like a good dose of popping and tick-tocking radiation to remind a person of the hard facts of life and death. Since embarking on this brain-tumor protocol, I have been forced to consider thoughts I've been avoiding for much of my adult life. Chemotherapy and radiation therapy have been the catalysts to allow myself to think in ways I haven't thought before. In that radiating moment, I realized I had to begin writing this shit down. So, here goes.

Cancer, like a lot of things in nature, is a selfish bitch. It sucks out your life and gives you nothing in return. These writings will remedy that to a small degree.

Some people feel sorry for me. A really nice lady came up to me in the local mini-mart the other day and gave me a long hug. She wouldn't let me go. "You mean so much to this community. Promise to let me know if you need anything," she said. She was sweet, so I didn't mind too much. We were right in front of the red wine selection. As the embrace continued, my mind began to wander. *Should I grab a bottle of Chilean Malbec for my wife? Then again, Lana loves beer too. Maybe a six-pack of that highbrow beer, Stella Artois.*

"Thank you. I appreciate that. I will definitely let you know if we need anything," I heard myself say. *I better get her a twelve-pack. And Sambuca for me.*

I understand the sympathy from dear friends like this, and it encourages me.

Here's what isn't encouraging: Christians who say they're praying for me. I'm not sure what their prayers accomplish. Probably nothing. I like to think I live in the real world, where prayer doesn't do anything—except make the praying person feel better. So, when people say they're praying for me, it seems like it's about them, not me.

From what I understand, brain tumors can never be eradicated or miraculously cured. Cancer is selfish. Even at the cost of their host, glioma tumors will grow and take over. They can merely be beaten back, like I beat back the weeds in my lawn. Those selfish dandelions always come back.

But I'm okay with a lack of supernatural healing. I don't feel entitled to a life of comfort and ease.

Apparently, this new treatment will add six years to my life. Not bad, if you ask me. What price would you pay to add six years to your life? One thousand years ago, people would have considered radiation therapy magic and my technicians wizards.

I was bullshitting with a young woman at the pub where I work about customers who complain about the food. We agreed it's wrong-headed to feel entitled to the best this world can offer. "Why complain about it? "she said, "Like having burnt fries or a shitty piece of naan bread is going to end their entire world?"

"I know, right?" I replied. "They're going to be really fucked when the world actually ends."

"Right," she responded awkwardly, shifting her gaze elsewhere.

Someone once asked me if having cancer motivates me to have a greater Christian impact in this world. To be honest, I don't care about Christian impact. If there's a god, that's his/her/its job. I feel too old. I've been trying to save the world as a pastor and missionary my entire adult life—almost twenty-five years. It's exhausting. Now I'm a bartender. It's also exhausting. So, I just try and get through each day, showing as much love and happiness as I can. The act of living can be 90 percent awesome, but that other 10 percent sure can take the piss out of you.

All our lives are ending. I just happen to know how mine will probably end. The two kid cooks at work want my liver and lungs when I die. One drinks too much, and one smokes too much. Yesterday, they even offered to pay for a tattoo that puts their names on my liver and lungs, claiming them after my funeral. It was a pretty funny request. "Not going to happen, you fuckers," I replied.

I think they tease me just to hear me say the word "fuckers." They like me and want to have some fun. Being minimum-wage cooks in a slow pub can be a shitty job, and laughter helps them pass the time. I really like those two kids. They know it too, and that's why they bullshit with me. When they're angry at the boss, I tell them to try forgiveness. Forgiveness from God is free. And the forgiveness we give to others is the only way to win a conflict. Holding onto resentment and bitterness is a dead-end road and a fickle lover.

I'm not sure what will happen to me during this next year of therapy. I've got to go through forty days and forty nights of radiation therapy, followed by a nine-month term of chemotherapy. The one thing I know is that I'll be documenting my thoughts throughout the experience. Let's call it thought therapy. I'm hoping that by the end of the birthing process, I'll have a sixty-thousand-word book for my children to read when they become adults.

There is no cure for brain tumors. And there may be no cure for my radiating thoughts and mutating beliefs. And I'm not sure I'd take the cure if one existed.

But hopefully, like a warm blanket got me through today's radiation therapy, this process of writing will help get me through this year of challenges.

DADDY SCHOOL

At work the other day, I accidentally bonked the chair of an elderly woman, who was sitting comfortably enjoying Sunday afternoon jazz. The result? Her tea spilled all over the table. I felt so bad, like I'd just stepped on the paw of a geriatric cat.

"I'm so sorry for bonking you. I really don't want to bonk you."

"I could take that personally, you know," said the elderly woman, a twinkle in her eye.

"Well, while I don't want to bonk you," I replied, after catching my breath, "maybe we could snuggle together after work?"

She blushed, and I went on with my job of pouring beer, serving hot wings, and making people smile. She was actually pretty cute...for a ninety-year-old.

The day before this bonking incident, in lieu of attending our local primary school (there was no school because of a teacher's strike), I decided that my kids, Hudson and Ellie, could learn a thing or two from me. We had what my kids call "Daddy School."

"Okay, kids, today's topic: God. Who wrote the Bible?"

"God?" the kids replied.

"Nope. A bunch of men who believe in God wrote it. Is everything in the Bible true?"

"Of course not, Dad."

"That's right," I said as I continued the lesson. "Is it possible for it to rain so much that Earth's entire surface is covered with water?"

"No."

"Is it possible to fit two of every type of animal on a large boat?"

"No."

"Then why do we read the Bible, if it's not all true?" I asked.

"We don't know, Dad."

"Have you heard the story of the Good Samaritan?"

"No."

"It's the story of a decent guy who got beat up by robbers," I explained.

At that point, Ellie got really excited. "Can we act it out? I'll be the robber, and Hudson can be the guy who gets beat up!"

"No, Ellie. So, anyway, the guy was left damaged on the side of the road. Then two church people walked by without helping him. Was that a nice thing to do?"

"No. That's mean," they said.

"Right," I agreed. "So, then a guy who nobody liked came by and helped the man."

"That's nice of him," the kids said.

"I know," I said, agreeing. "So, here's the question. Did that story really happen?"

"Nope. It's just a story."

"That's right. Did Jesus really tell that story?" I was getting close to my point. I could taste success.

"Maybe?"

"That's also right," I agreed again. "Maybe he did; maybe he didn't. The author believed that Jesus told it. What's the point of the Good Samaritan story?"

"Be nice to everyone, even people you don't like," they answered authoritatively.

"Exactly. Now here's the most important question of all: will you build your life on that idea and be nice to people, even if you don't like them?" I held my breath in anticipation.

"Yes!" the children shouted.

"And that's how we read the Bible," I said, bringing the excitement down a notch with my calm voice. "It doesn't matter if all the Bible is true. What matters is discovering the ideas in the Bible and deciding if you want to live that way or not."

"Can we play Minecraft now?" they asked, obviously tired of our talk.

"Yes," I replied. "Class dismissed. I'm going on strike now."

One of my favorite books is *There is No (A) God* by famous former atheist Antony Flew. In it he argues for the existence of a personal God. Not the God of the Bible or a Christian God. Just an omnipotent personal Other. Flew makes a thundering acknowledgement near the end of the book: "I think that the Christian religion is the one religion that most clearly deserves to be honored and respected whether or not its claim to be a divine revelation is true. There is nothing like the combination of a charismatic figure like Jesus and a first-class intellectual like St. Paul. If you're wanting Omnipotence to set up a religion, this is the one to beat."

I've decided to make a less-thundering but mildly crackling acknowledgement: "The real tragedy isn't that people don't believe the Bible but that people don't read it. If they did and managed to discover the point of some of the stories, their lives would be better."

We may even develop a sense of humor when clumsy people bonk us.

HOT TUB SPACESHIP

My neighbor builds houses by day and teaches ninja skills at night. He and my wife, Lana, have a mutual interest that involves neither hammers nor throwing stars. They both enjoy bugging me about my habit of going into my hot tub naked after dark.

"Dude," he says, "you're like a six-foot-four-inch piece of white paper. Just because your deck lights are off doesn't mean people can't see you. You're probably brighter than the moon."

"I think you're just jealous," I reply.

To which Lana says, "You're going to freak out our retired neighbors!"

"I don't think they can see me," I say, "but even if they could, so what? Consider it my gift to them."

I go into my hot tub on a nightly basis for two reasons, and neither has anything to do with my naturalist views.

1. The jets give me a killer massage.

2. I like to imagine I'm a space traveler.

The planet my hot tub sits on is rotating at five hundred meters per second. This rotating planet is circling around the sun at about one hundred kilometers per second. Earth and the sun, along with every other planet and star in the Milky Way, are speeding toward the Great Attractor (a conglomeration of about eight thousand galaxies) at about two hundred kilometers per second. And all these galaxies are, in turn, hurtling toward the Shapley Supercluster at about three hundred kilometers per second. It's like I'm driving a speedboat around in circles in a swimming pool, which is on a cruise ship that is speeding around in circles in a bigger swimming pool, which is on a bigger cruise ship, which is circling around in a much larger swimming pool on an even larger cruise ship, which is also speeding around in circles in an even bigger pool on an even bigger boat traveling toward a watery infinity.

See why I feel like a space traveler?

I recently added Edwin's former hit song, "Another Spin Around the Sun," to my computer. I remember shedding a tear or two listening to it on a CD in my car back in 2002. I had just ended a difficult relationship with a church at which I loved working. My brain tumor was just an evil baby then, having been diagnosed the previous year. I was still in denial regarding its deadly nature and kept telling people it was merely a cyst. That song meant the world to me.

Ain't it good to be alive?
Another spin around the sun
On this speck of light in the universe
A little piece of love is in everyone.

Did you know the light from the stars that I look at from my hot tub shone their light at me between 50 and 250 years ago? That's how long it took their light to reach my naked eyes. I'm looking at antique sunlight from stars much bigger than our sun.

Does this make you feel small? Not me. I feel big. I'm alive in this huge universe, aware of things too fantastic than I deserve to be aware of. Do you know how tiny the chance of life being able to evolve on our planet is? If Earth was a few centimeters closer to the sun, it'd be too hot to sustain life.

If it was a few centimeters farther from our little sun, it'd be too cold to sustain life. If our spinning and hurtling were off by a few kilometres per second, life, as we know it, would not have developed.

Small? No way. I live on a planet of giants. And it is good to be alive. I have been given an opportunity to shine brightly. Sometimes even brighter than the moon.

THE QUEEN OF CROFTON

A regular customer at the pub tells me that she feels entitled to everything she can get and that I should too. She explained her views quite clearly to me the other day: "The squeaky wheel gets the oil. So, I squeak as much as I can."

Here are three of her more memorable squeaks.

If it's bright in the pub: "This is a bar, not a cafeteria. This pub has absolutely no atmosphere."

If the front doors are open: "Close that door. I'm hot and want the air conditioning on."

If there's a jug of water on the bar counter: "Who's the idiot who put the water jug on the bar? I'm here to drink beer, not water."

I asked her if she was the Queen of Crofton. She said she was. Then she told me that I also deserved whatever I could get out of life. I laughed and heard myself blurt, "I don't deserve shit."

I was already feeling tired from driving to Victoria each morning and sluggish from the daily radiation therapy. On top of that, I had received a speeding ticket that day for going forty-four kilometers over the speed limit on the highway. The officer explained how he had my fine dropped from $600 and a seven-day impounding to a mere $197. I had to bite my tongue from thanking him inappropriately for his kindness.

I have a bad person squirming around inside me trying to get out. Sorry, Mr. Officer.

I'm not complaining. Just giving you context for what popped out of my mouth as I continued my stream-of-consciousness conversation with the Queen of Crofton: "I don't deserve shit. I have discovered the secret to contentment, and it's not about thinking I deserve more. Whether I have lots or just a little, I can be content. Being a squeaky wheel would only make me miserable."

"It gets me what I want," she said.

"But isn't the squeaky wheel the first wheel to be replaced?" I countered.

I used to think more highly of myself than I ought. For instance, I remember working at a summer camp when I was twenty. I was under the impression that the kids in my cabin were as enamored with me as I was. At the end of the week, I learned otherwise.

"We had a lot of fun, didn't we?" I said to my campers.

"It was okay," they replied.

"I guess having me as your camp counsellor really made the week awesome, right?"

"You were fun, but we'll probably forget about you tomorrow," one kid said.

"Yeah," another kid added. "Life will go on just fine without you in our lives."

"Oh," I said dejectedly.

Talk about letting the air out of my squeaky tires.

I used to pride myself on being the first kid in the pool, the lake, or river. In terms of life experiences, I've always been a few strokes ahead of the kids with whom I grew up. I've traveled more, met more famous people, and attempted more than most I've known. I thought I was important because of that.

Later in life I was talking to a recruitment officer at a large church in Atlanta. By the end of our conversation, I realized I wasn't who I thought I was.

"Tell me about yourself," said the hiring officer.

"I'm a visionary leader," I said proudly, just as I had practiced.

"Can I be blunt with you?" he asked.

"Please do," I said hesitantly.

"I could tell as soon as I met you that you're not a visionary leader. Maybe you can lead a Bible study someday." He started to greet the next guy in line.

"But I've always been the first one in the pool," I pleaded.

He turned to me one last time. "What good is being the first in the pool if you're not a good swimmer?"

I was devastated. I felt like I was drowning. But soon I began to agree with him. I was not a visionary leader.

Did I stop trying to be a pastor? No. I became a better pastor. A humbled pastor. I owe that guy for being so painfully honest with me. I am not as important as I once thought.

And I don't deserve shit.

After the Queen of Crofton paid for her two beers and side of fries, she left. As I opened the doors, turned on the bright lights, and put the water back on the bar counter, I thought about our culture. There's a false religion in our world that isn't atheism or militant Islam or, worse, evangelical Christianity. It's people who believe they're basically good and entitled to more. It's not true. We all have a bad person inside trying to get out.

The people I want to spend my time with aren't the entitled people of this world. It's the people who try their best to smother their bad inner self by humbly showing kindness to others. The contented wheel gets far more oil than the squeaky wheel, simply because it needs less oil.

The Queen of Crofton returned a few days later. She had a card for the servers at the pub: "People express themselves in many beautiful and wonderful ways. Me? I bitch."

It was a great moment of realized truth; I realized how much I love our Queen. God save the Queen. God save us all.

THE CIRCLE OF HEALING

I was sitting in my hot tub the other day smoking some medicinal marijuana. Hey, gotta try everything once. Well, not everything. But if it's medicinal, then maybe.

Maybe you're wondering who rolled my joint. My wife did. Who knew? That's a skill set I didn't know she had when I married her. You think you know a person, right? Thanks for the Saturday Night Special, Lana.

[Editor's note: Lana can roll it but doesn't roll with it. This was a solo mission.]

Where did I get my weed? Good question. I got it as a tip from some customers who import and sell medicinal marijuana. This particular batch was from Bob Marley's estate in Jamaica. It's called Lamb's Bread. Sounds like church communion, right? How can that be bad? The medicinal ingredients in Lamb's Bread are known to improve creativity, increase energy, and boost personal happiness. I was sure it was going to be a win/win/win.

This was not the first time I'd tried this type of medicine. The first time it had no effect on me either. Lana says it was because I was hammered at the time, but I just figured I had an immunity to weed. Or maybe it was the fact I only had one little puff. Either way, I'm not a quitter. So, in the comfort of my hot tub, I tried again. But it still wasn't working. I was so disappointed with the dud bud that I chucked it out of the tub and onto the ground. I was feeling entitled to my improved creativity, increased energy, and boosted personal happiness. And nothing.

There's something I haven't told you: I've been getting pot-smoking lessons from Kid Cook, who works at the pub with me. The kid who wants my liver when I die. He's been telling me that the trick to smoking medicinal marijuana is holding the smoke in longer. So, that's what I'd been trying to do, to no avail. All I got for my efforts was a sore throat and a burning cough.

And then I saw it. As I looked up into the night sky around midnight in my hot tub with what was left of that Jamaican joint languishing on the ground beside me, I saw a vision. The smoke from the neighboring pulp mill began to change into the shape of a rubber ducky's head. The ducky's head popped out of the stars right at me, like an image on my 3D television. Then the other clouds and mill smoke began to change shape into other 3D animals, like crocodiles, puppies, and even tractors. They all gathered around the rubber ducky's head in what seemed like a healing circle. It was so beautiful.

And then it all made sense to me. I had achieved clarity. There were two lessons for me this night. The first lesson was so simple: I'm not immune after all.

And the second lesson? One day, if I'm patient, I may just receive healing too.

THE WAVE

This morning as I was heading to Victoria for my daily radiation therapy, I had a good chat with my daughter, who I was dropping off at childcare. We were driving past the striking teachers, and I suggested to Ellie that we wave to our teaching friends, like we always do. So, we did. Striking teachers are the friendliest bystanders I've ever seen.

"Daddy," Ellie wondered aloud, "if we wave to the teachers, does it mean we're agreeing with them and their reasons for striking?"

"Do you agree with the teachers?" I asked after a brief pause.

"I don't know. But I love them. And they wouldn't know that if I didn't wave to them."

I smiled. My daughter has figured it out. I said it doesn't matter if the teachers think we agree with them or not. What's important is that they know we love them.

Ellie doesn't understand why the schools aren't open. She has no understanding of Provision E80 and the effect it has on class sizes and composition. Nor does she know that Jim Iker is the union leader and that Christy Clark is the provincial government leader.

But she knows her heart. And above all, she wants to share what's in her heart with others. She hasn't lost that yet. So what if her love is misunderstood as agreement? Where's the harm in that? The real harm is holding back our love for fear of it being misunderstood as insecurity, weakness, or agreement.

Someone asked me the other day if I believed God was in my life. I *think* God is in my life, but who knows for sure? I'm not convinced God is in my life in a specific way or if he ever was. I used to stand up and claim that God led me to go here or there or to believe this or that.

I've stood in front of church congregations while people claimed with certainty that God brought me there, and then, a couple of years later, the same people claimed with certainty that God wanted me to leave. Claiming to have certainty about God's involvement or leading or whatever seems more like a mental illness than faith. How can a person speak for God and know his mind?

So, is God in my life? No. Not in a specific way. But here's where I do see God in my life in a general way: in people. When people choose love as their guiding principle, positive change always happens in their lives and in the lives of those around them. Call me mental, but I'm certain of it.

So, yes, I believe love is in my life. And love comes from God, for God must be love if God is anything. And this morning in the car on my way to radiation therapy, love was sitting behind me in a booster seat...waving at her teachers.

MORALISTS

After a concert at the pub the other day, a day in which I was exhausted from serving more customers than I'd ever served in my short two-month career as a bartender, I was cleaning up the many dirty tables, while the other servers went out for a smoke break. I'm seriously considering becoming a smoker, simply so I can get more breaks. Only four customers were left in the pub, and they were all sitting at the front corner table by the window. I'd characterize the four gentlemen as badasses. You know, like cowboys, or bikers. Or mill workers. They were in their fifties and not the type of fellows with whom I'd have instant chemistry. Not yet anyway. I'm still working on being more of a badass.

As I was cleaning the table next to theirs, I inadvertently overheard bits of their conversation. They were talking about conflicts around the globe, war, and the end of the world. Being as tired as I was, I had less control over my tongue than usual, and I sprang a verbal leak. "Repent, sinner," I announced. "The end is near."

They took my comment in stride and began talking to me about the pettiness of requiring repentance to go to heaven.

"What Jesus did by dying for us was powerful enough to get forgiveness for everyone, regardless of our repentance," I said. "We don't repent for God's benefit but for our own. There's freedom in acknowledging to God that we're all assholes."

Then my badass friends chimed in again, agreeing that they knew deep down they were indeed assholes. They didn't have any problem with that particular point of theology. Until one of the guys changed his opinion.

"I'm actually a really good person," the righteous badass said. "But these guys, they're the real assholes."

We all had a good laugh, and I continued cleaning up the empty beer bottles from the remaining fifteen dirty tables while my new badass friends went outside to have a smoke with my co-workers.

One of the reasons I stopped attending church over a year ago is because every church I've been to is full of moralists. A moralist is someone who places an exaggerated sense of importance on what is right behavior and what is wrong behavior.

Here are three examples:

1. A church dad who is disappointed with me for baptizing a young mother who is living with the father of her daughter but is not married to him.

2. A church leader who is upset with me for suggesting we allow a young lesbian to help with youth group leadership.

3. A church person who is shocked at me for telling off-color jokes at an open-mike comedy night at the local pub.

I know details about each of these people's lives that would reveal to you that they are no more moral than the three people they were claiming were immoral.

Classic hypocrisy.

Moralists are hypocrites who not only infiltrate churches and destroy the sense of community there but also exist all around us in society. The parent who complains that all teachers are greedy is a moralist. The person up the street who complains about the pot-smoking neighbor is a moralist. The child who tells me that another child always cheats at Junior Monopoly is a budding moralist.

A moralist believes he or she is better than other people, because the moralist behaves better. In the church world, the implication is that God likes the moralist more as a result. It's simply not true.

Jesus' friends tell us that Jesus was the only person who ever lived who was qualified to be a moralist. But he never acted like one. Ironically, the people who liked Jesus the most were the badasses of his day, not the hypocritical religious people. Andy Stanley, my favorite preacher, often says that people who were nothing like Jesus liked Jesus.

Jesus wasn't a moralist. I don't want to be a moralist either. I know my heart. I can be a real asshole. That is very accurate.

What would it take for me to begin attending church again? Simple. Show me a church that's full of assholes like me.

Part Two

TIME TRAVEL

I can feel it building up inside

The images that play inside my mind

Dreams that I've been dreaming all my life

The colors that live outside of the lines

But dreams aren't all I hide beneath this skin

The cord is cut, the fears and doubts begin

My hope is anchored on the other side

With the colors that live outside of the lines

And the oceans roar

And the wheel's in spin

And the old chorus soars

Bring me back, bring me back to the beginning again

—SWITCHFOOT

TIME TRAVELLING ON A
SUNDAY MORNING

I woke the kids up early this morning.

"We're going to time travel today, kids," I said.

"Really?" they replied.

"Yup. We're going to visit an Orthodox Church."

Services at Orthodox churches are as ancient as you can get. They're still performing rituals that Christians performed in the third century. It's like time-traveling. So, off we went to the city of Parksville to St. Mary the Protectress Ukrainian Orthodox Church. The only other Orthodox church on Vancouver Island is in Victoria, and I go to Victoria enough already for radiation therapy. We arrived ten minutes late and took our place with the other twenty people in attendance. All the readings were sung acapella, not read. It was melodious, which was cool. There were neat pictures everywhere. They call them icons. Pictures of Jesus, saints, and famous holy warriors. The OCD part of me started scheming how I could get my own collection of those kaleidoscopic pictures.

I really wanted to enjoy my time at this Orthodox church, but I didn't. There's a reason only twenty people attend.

The priest told us this next story to explain the feast day on which we had arrived, the Feast of the Universal Exaltation of the Precious and Life-giving Cross. According to this black-cloaked, middle-aged white man, in 326 C.E., the Christian

Roman emperor, Constantine, sent his mother, Helen, to Jerusalem to find the cross on which Jesus died. After some investigation, Helen discovered not only the cross of Calvary but also the two crosses that flanked Jesus on that skull-shaped hill. Not knowing which cross was the real one, Helen had a leprous woman brought in. This sick woman kissed the first two crosses, with no effect. Then, as she kissed the third cross, she was miraculously healed. The true cross had been found. This cross was lifted up, or exalted, before a great crowd of people and subsequently celebrated through annual feasts.

I find most of this story hard to believe. And yet the priest told this story as if it was the most truthful information he'd heard in his life. It's probably true that Helen visited Jerusalem and made some important archaeological discoveries, but the rest requires much more faith than I can muster. I haven't been brain-damaged enough to believe fairy tales yet. (Though I am told that since my radiation therapy began two weeks ago, I have a real glow about me.)

The problem I have with most organized religion is the glaring lack of humility. The leaders of most churches claim with certainty that ridiculous stories are true. Whether we're talking about the human race propagating from a literal Adam and Eve, a loving God commanding the genocide of Canaanite women and children so his chosen people could colonize Palestine, or the miraculous healing powers of a cross-shaped chunk of wood, most religious stories are too nonsensical to be true. If these stories were factual, then the God I've been trying to love all my life is more like a silly toddler with a weird imagination than a beautiful, loving Creator.

According to the story the Orthodox priest told us today, after the cross was exalted, the crowd responded in humility: "Lord, have mercy."

Finally, something I can agree with.

ISRAEL

I was bullshitting with an Israeli woman and her Buddhist husband the other day in the pub. She was asking about my experiences in Israel two years ago. I went to Israel in place of my dad. Let me explain.

My father was born in 1937 on a German Mennonite commune in the former Soviet Union. Stalin treated Mennonites like shit, so most fled during the Nazi withdrawal of 1944. During my dad's escape from the horrors of war, his father, my grandfather, whom I never met, was separated from the family, eventually believing his family to be dead. He remarried and started a new family in the Ukraine. My dad ended up in Canada and never saw his father again.

I always loved hearing my dad tell this story. I don't know why. Maybe it helped give this Vancouver Island boy a sense of history. A sense of place. A sense of identity. As I got older, my dad and I had a recurring conversation about his childhood home. "Dad," I'd often ask, "would you like to go to the Ukraine and visit where you grew up?" He'd always reply, "No, not really." Unperturbed, I'd always answer, "But you have family there. You have half-brothers and half-sisters you've never met." And invariably he'd reply, "That doesn't interest me. You know where I would like to visit? Israel. Someday, I'd like to visit the place where Jesus lived."

My father never went to Israel. So, after he died, I did.

I started talking with my new pub friends about my two favorite places that my dad never visited: the Church of Saint Peter's House in Capernaum and the Church of the Holy Sepulcher in Jerusalem.

Why are these my two favorite places in Israel, the place where Jesus slept on his buddy's couch in Capernaum and the place where Jesus died and was buried in Jerusalem? Because archeologists have found proof that Jesus was secretly worshipped as God in both places in the first century. According to our tour guide, a secular Jew, the fact that Jewish people secretly worshipped Jesus as God in these places puts the historicity of these locations beyond doubt. There's no reason to think Jesus lived or died elsewhere if people were putting their lives on the line to worship him in these two places. According to our tour guide, it is a historical certainty that Jesus lived in Capernaum and died in Jerusalem and that they worshipped him as God there.

Why would Jewish people worship a human as God? As bizarre as that sounds, the archeological discoveries are hard to dispute. Something happened two thousand years ago to change people's minds about the appropriateness of worshipping Jesus as God, a practice unheard of culturally and against the law of the day.

My new pub friends had never heard about the significance of these places before.

"Have you ever read the stories of Jesus?" I asked them.

"No," she responded. "I would never read the New Testament."

"You make it sound like it's hate literature," I countered. "I think the gospels demand to be read. Sure, they've been heavily edited. And yes, parts are racist and misogynist, but there's also a golden thread of divinity there. One doesn't have to touch the New Testament to enjoy them. Just look these books up on the internet."

"Hmm," they said. "Maybe we will."

I tried to explain to her that no other first-century documents are as exciting, readable, and surprising as these writings. She could read how Jesus raised all sorts of hell. He broke the biggest rules of the day when he embraced infectious women, touched defiled corpses, and even spent time with worthless children. Best of all, whenever Jesus encountered manipulative religion, he lost his shit. He flipped tables and called the religious leaders maggot-infested hypocrites. And apparently, he did all these things to secure forgiveness and free access to God for everyone who wanted it.

"Do you believe that people who don't worship Jesus are going to hell?" one of them asked me.

"No," I said. "Of course not; that's childish and manipulative."

She was happy to hear this, in the same way a person would be happy to discover their new friend is not a member of the Branch Davidians or the Ku Klux Klan.

I remember singing the Jeremy Riddle song, "Sweetly Broken," under my breath as I knelt in that Catholic church in Jerusalem to kiss the place where Jesus died.

> *To the cross I look, and to the cross I cling.*
> *Of its suffering, I do drink; Of its work, I do sing.*
> *On it, my Savior, both bruised and crushed*
> *Showed that God is love and God is just.*

My father understood the significance of these places he'd never visited. My Jewish friend lived next door to these places but had no idea of their significance. And me? I've come to realize that my identity isn't in the Ukraine with a lost extended family. Whether I like it or not, my identity remains inexplicably linked to that person who was secretly worshipped as God in the first century.

IDOLIZING THE BIBLE

Some people ask me how I justify picking and choosing which parts of the Bible to believe. Good question.

Before I explain myself, I think it's important to point out that every Christian picks and chooses what parts of the Bible they prefer. When I was ending my employment at my last church, several people picked and chose certain Bible verses with which to shame me. Verses about good pastors not drinking (I drink), not swearing (I swear), and not getting mad (I get mad). Yet these same people ignored other verses they didn't like. One person disliked and ignored the verses about water baptism. Another disliked and ignored the verses about eternal torment. A third disliked and ignored the verses about substitutionary atonement (the belief that Jesus died instead of us). My point isn't to humiliate these types of people but merely to show that every Christian picks and chooses.

The Bible contains many stories that are too far-fetched to believe. Many commandments that are too oppressive to obey. Many beliefs that are too narrow to adopt. I refuse to follow such verses any longer.

The belief that the entire Bible is inspired and without error is called biblical inerrancy. The debate about biblical inerrancy is fairly recent, coming to a head merely sixty or so years ago. Prior to that, it wasn't as big a deal to not believe in the divine inspiration of the entire Bible. In fact, I could show you lots of places in the New Testament where the writers pick and choose what Old Testament verses to believe and focus on and which verses not to believe and not to focus on.

To believe the entire Bible as true requires us to be against divorce, gay marriage, women teaching in church, and over-eating, not to mention Harry Potter, Yoda, and Gandalf. (Wizards are forbidden in the Bible.) I choose to interpret the Bible with an imagination.

I once heard Michael Palin, of Monty Python fame, describe the problem with organized religion: "The guys who started many of our world religions were imaginative thinkers, but most of their followers weren't. As a result, the followers would often take something metaphorical or poetic and make it a literal rule, thus often reaching the opposite conclusion of the original leader's main point."

(Blessed are the cheesemakers? What's so special about the cheesemakers?)

Some people ask me if I'll ever work in a church again. I'd like to, but I doubt it'll ever happen. Why? Because most of the churches that are hiring demand a belief in biblical iner-rancy before they'll consider someone. It's a shame, really. It elevates the Bible above God. When *I* pick and choose, I'm simply choosing God first.

PUNCHING DOLPHINS

The other day as I drove to radiation therapy in Victoria, I was listening to a review of *Dolphin Tale 2* on the radio. The reviewer said the movie was so bad it made him want to hate dolphins. He said that after watching it, he felt like punching a dolphin in the face.

I bet a lot of people feel the same way about Jesus. Maybe they watched *The Passion of the Christ* or went to a boring church service and left feeling like they wanted to punch Jesus in the face. I don't think anyone really wants to punch Jesus—or a dolphin—in the face; they're just angry with the person who made the bad movie or preached the bad sermon.

When *The Passion* came out, the church I was attending bought up hundreds of tickets for the congregation to invite their friends to go see the movie with them. The hope was that as our friends witnessed Mel Gibson's ultra-violent vision of Jesus' torture, they would realize the love of God and the depth of their sin, thus receiving Jesus into their hearts as their Lord and Savior while sitting in the movie theater. I refused to participate in the campaign. It seemed crooked, like a great way to fill Mel Gibson's bank account. Besides, no one converts because of a movie. So, instead I took my friends to see the movie *Hellboy*, which came out the same weekend. It's about a multi-dimensional demon trying to be a good Christian superhero. My favorite scene is near the end, when Hellboy is beginning to embrace his demonic side. His friend tosses a crucifix necklace to Hellboy. After he catches it, the pendant marks his hand with the image of the cross. Christ, not Satan, is the source of Hellboy's true identity. Better movie than *The Passion.*

I was at a funeral service a few years ago where the pastor attempted to shame the children and other family members into accepting Christ, so they could see their beloved mother again in heaven. I was mortified.

"If you ever want to see your dead mother again, you must believe in Jesus right now," he preached.

Give her kids guns, and you have the makings of a great Quentin Tarantino movie.

I have a friend who once confided to me that church makes her feel very uncomfortable, because people speak so emotionally and intimately about Jesus. About how much they love him. About how much he loves them. About how he wants to hug them or cry with them or sing lullabies to them or give them a wet, sloppy kiss. *Please, get a room!* She wrote to me in an email. *That's personal! Keep that to yourself! I also don't want to hear the details of your sex life!*

I have a T-shirt with a picture of Jesus on it, arms open wide. The caption reads: "Come at me bro! Matthew 11:28." I wore it to the rock 'n' roll bingo night at the pub, and some drunk women took note.

"That's a fucking rad shirt!" they said.

They wanted to take a picture of me. Of course, I obliged. They liked the idea of Jesus welcoming them with open arms at the pub.

People like Jesus. They also like dolphins. Let's not make it easy for them to want to punch either in the face.

108 BILLION CHILDREN

I was in my hot tub the other night trying to distract myself from the fact that radiation therapy was making my hair fall out in clumps, so I began thinking about how many people have lived on this planet. Of course, estimating how many human beings have ever lived, including prehistoric populations, involves some guesswork, but the best estimates I've read are around 108 billion. Actually, that's the only estimate I read. It was raining, and I didn't want my iPhone to get wet.

If all 108 billion of us are children of God, then God has a lot of kids. And based on what I know about God, God must love all his kids. That's a lot of kids to love, but Lana tells me that love is like air, so God can easily love them all.

That's cool that everyone is a child of God. There is beauty in that thought. But I don't always appreciate it. You see, there's also something bad in me - a bad seed that keeps me from God's parenting. I tend to prefer being at the center of my own world and too often focus my energies on myself; like I'm God's child, but I prefer to live in foster care most of the time. My foster parents seem nice, but they're actually not very good. They basically let me follow my natural inclinations. And that gets me in trouble. Many of my natural inclinations make for poor guidance counsellors, let alone parents.

I grew up believing the only way for me, or anyone, to be adopted back into God's family was through repentance. I remember when the book *The Purpose-Driven Life* came out and the author was shit-kicked by certain Christians for not using the word "repent" enough. He didn't use it at all, actually. *The Purpose-Driven Life* is the second-most-translated book in the world, after the Bible.

So, as I was pulling out clumps of hair and trying not to clog up the hot tub filter, I realized that bit of theology is ridiculous. If I were the father of 108 billion children who lived in a shitty foster-care system, I would not wait for them to repent before I adopted them back into my family. I would create a system where they could all be adopted back in at the same time, whether they realized it or not.

We adopted our daughter, Ellie, into our family at the age of ten months. For the first ten months of her life, she was our foster baby. But from her perspective, we're the only mommy and daddy she's ever known. She was loved and then adopted into our family without even realizing it had happened. Why couldn't God do the same thing?

I've been rereading the stories of Jesus, and it sure seems to me that's exactly what God did. Today I read how someone asked Jesus: "What are you all about?" Jesus replied: "I came to get important shit done." Well, that's how I translate the actual words in the text: "I came to seek and save the lost."

But after he saved us all, Jesus left. He wrote no books, painted no pictures. He didn't build a single church building. In fact, a lot of the time he told people to just hush up about him. It was like he *knew* he was going to be misunderstood. As if he'd created a system that would not depend on anyone getting his story straight afterwards or on people repenting properly. It's like he made a way for all 108 billion of us to be adopted back into God's family, even if it seemed like many of us were still living in foster care.

Someone much smarter than me once asked if we could be justified by faith without believing in justification by faith.

Why is this important to me? Because I need God to be bigger than a simplistic deity who holds back his love until I say I'm sorry. If I can think of a way for him to do that (and I'm not that bright), I'm sure he can too, and I believe he did.

Tonight at rock 'n' roll bingo, I was quizzing the people at the pub about certain songs I'd been playing for them.

"What was the song I just played?" I asked.

"'Santa Maria' by Trooper!" the crowd yelled.

"What does Santa Maria mean in English?"

"Santa Claus's wife?" a woman in the crowd asked hesitantly.

"No. It means Saint Mary," I said. "Now who is Saint Mary?"

"God's mom!" someone else cried out.

"Close enough," I said. "Now what is this song? It's about the war to end all wars…"

"'Armageddon' by Prism!" someone else hollered, proudly.

"That's right. What book of the Bible is Armageddon from?"

"Revelation!" the same guy yelled confidently.

"Right again," I replied. "But who wrote Revelation?"

The hesitant woman spoke again. "God?"

"Nope," I said. "Some dude named John. God didn't write the Bible."

"Oh well," she said dejectedly, "I'm just a sinner then."

"Fortunately for us, Jesus liked sinners best," I replied.

"Yay! Now play some more songs. This is a pub, not Sunday School!" the confident guy yelled at me.

Jesus once said he didn't come to condemn his 108 billion brothers and sisters but to save them. I'm glad he did. Whether most of us realize it or not.

BROKEN PIECES

The other day, my son, Hudson, came home telling me that he broke his record. He ran fourteen laps in the Terry Fox Run for Cancer. Last year, he ran only ten. I looked at him and noticed a sticker on the front of his hoodie. It read: "Terry Fox ran for me. I'm running for my dad."

Why would Hudson run for me? I don't have cancer. Then I remembered. Shit. I do. Why else would I drive to Victoria every morning for radiation therapy? I started to tear up. I am so proud of Hudson and Ellie. It must be difficult for them to have a broken daddy who doesn't even admit to himself that he's broken most of the time.

A long-time friend named Juliet makes art from broken pieces of glass. She sent me the script for a sermon she preached recently at her church: "We don't like broken things. We like to fix them or throw them away. But when I think of the things I like most in the world, they are broken things: shards of colored glass or tile, rocks, sand, and glitter. My imagination wants to re-form them intuitively into something new, something even better."

I'm loving the *Fading West* album by Switchfoot. It's also a movie on Netflix. My second-favorite song on the album is "Back to the Beginning Again." (My favorite song is "Saltwater Heart.")

And my heart is yours
And what a broken place it's in.
But you're what I'm running for
And I want to feel the wind at my back again.

Hudson, Ellie, and I went to Bike Works this past summer in Duncan. It's a non-profit society that collects old, broken bikes and recycles them. Hudson and I built a BMX bike for him while Ellie painted and drew pictures of crooked fairies and slant-eyed princesses. Afterwards, they let me take an adult bike home for myself. I love riding it. It reminds me of my childhood, riding down Venlaw Road in Nanaimo. Sometimes I think riding a bike is the closest thing I'll ever feel to flying. I love feeling the wind in my face and at my back.

Juliet's sermon went on: "Before Jesus meets his death, he has a supper and breaks bread, sharing it with his friends, a group of imperfect people. He says to eat the bread that is broken and the wine that is poured out in remembrance of his broken body and his spilled blood...Perhaps if we can accept our brokenness as a gift, a sign of our completeness, we will find that we are more whole than we ever were before we accepted it."

I'm not sure if that's true, that our brokenness is a gift to remind us that, through acceptance, we become more complete, but it's a nice thought, don't you think?

But then again, if brokenness is a gift, maybe it's time for God to stop giving us presents.

GETTING CUT OFF

I told my kids that when I die, I'm going to donate my brain to science, because I'm a genius, and my face to charity, because I'm so good looking. They asked what would sit atop my neck in the coffin. Lana suggested we could use a pumpkin. Then they started to argue about who would get to carve it.

Some people ask me how I know when to cut people off at the bar. Do I make them walk a line or wait for them to start a fight? It's much easier than that. I cut them off as soon as they start crying about how bad their life is.

When I hear someone say, "I'm such a terrible person!" I cut them off.

"I don't have any friends!" I cut them off.

"My life is such a waste!" I cut them off.

(After noticing my radiation baldness) "What the fuck happened to your hair? Did you lose a bet?" I cut them all off.

It's predictable how alcohol affects certain people. And it's amazing to me how blind people can be about how they behave. Don't they see that they go through the same emotions each time they drink? They start out happy and end up crying about the same things as the night before and the night before that. It's like a script they pull out of their pockets to recite again and again. They're rehearsing a play they'll never actually perform. Lana tells me they just need a friend. I disagree. We all have friends. What the drunks at the bar need is the same thing I need: conversion to hope.

Carl Jung, the renowned psychiatrist, once said that the great neurosis of our time is emptiness.

I don't believe our world was created to sustain us. That's why no matter how much stuff we buy, we still feel empty. No matter how much we drink, we still feel thirsty. Our world was created to point us to something bigger than us. Once we see our own insignificance and become converted to hope, many of our self-sustaining tears dry up.

Someone once said that if you can't find conversion for yourself, then you need to at least rub up against the heart of someone who has been converted. Maybe that's why people pour out their pain in bars. Or read books like this.

Ever since my kids could understand words, I've told them the most important thing is to tell God their feelings. It takes faith to tell God our feelings. It also takes courage to face our feelings of loss, doubt, and emptiness. But once we begin sharing them, they often dissipate. Just float away. We get served a pint of hope. We don't need to keep repeating the scripts. God is the ultimate bartender. And he never cuts us off.

MESSING WITH SANTA

I've always taught my kids that while Santa Claus isn't real, it's a fun game to play at Christmas time. They've always seemed to appreciate my candor and the fun of me dressing up as Santa Claus on December 25. This skinny, red-suited man would try to convince them that their dad was lying and that he was the real Santa. Santa would also tell the kids that their dad was probably out having a smoke or doing some gardening and would be back later in the day.

I told that story in church once as part of a sermon. It was the most trouble I've ever gotten into for a sermon. I've preached on hell not existing, and I've preached that suits and ties aren't necessary for true believers but never received as much backlash as the time I went against Santa. I apologized the next Sunday for ruining people's Christmas and stated publicly that I may have been wrong about Santa not being real, because I had seen him at the mall the day before.

The most trouble I've gotten into with parents at the local school was when my kids attempted to tell their friends that Santa wasn't real. The small-town gossip mill really started churning out the buttery bile that time. To keep the pitchfork-and-shotgun-toting, quad-riding villagers at bay, I've taught my children to just smile and nod when their friends talk about their belief in Santa.

The moral of the story: don't mess with Santa.

After reading *The God Delusion* by Richard Dawkins, I began talking to my kids differently about God. Dawkins argues that parents should not automatically indoctrinate their children with their beliefs. So, instead of saying, "We believe in Jesus" or "Our family believes in heaven," I'd say, "Your daddy believes in Jesus" and "Your daddy believes in heaven."

It turns out that Hudson doesn't exactly agree with Dawkins.

"Dad," Hudson said, "I know it's what you believe. You don't have to say that all the time. I usually just believe what you believe anyway."

One time when I was being interviewed for a church job, the hiring committee asked me two short questions, and after my great answers, they were about to end the interview and hire me. But I interrupted them, "Is that it? No other questions?"

"Okay then," the committee chair said. "Is there anything else you'd like to tell us?"

"Um, okay," I began. "In the interest of full disclosure, you should know that I believe that Charles Darwin was right about evolution. And not just about evolution within a species but about big evolution too. He was right that we all come from a common ancestor. That we share almost all the same DNA as rats, monkeys, and even yeast. That Adam and Eve crawled out of the primordial ooze as amazing one-celled creatures, and that every other living creature evolved from them."

"Well," the chair said, without missing a beat, "as long as you don't talk about that to anyone, we don't see it as a problem." One committee member stated that she agreed with me but had never heard anyone in church say it out loud before.

One guy who attended the same church had left his previous church, because the pastor said in a sermon that anyone who believed Earth was only ten thousand years old was being naive and a bad witness. I didn't realize how easily offended my friend was.

"Dude," I told him, "anyone who believes that Earth is only ten thousand years old *is* being naive and a bad witness. (I patted him on the back.) But I'd never say that publicly."

I feel bad for kids who believe in religious fairy tales like these and end up at university and have their faith torn apart by intelligent professors in a matter of minutes. The tape cassettes I used to try to get my high school friends to listen to in order to convince them that the reason dinosaurs didn't exist was because Noah couldn't fit them on the ark would not convince a lab rat, let alone a microbiologist with a PhD. Whether it's golden tablets from heaven, blue gods with eight arms, or a literal six-day creation, intelligent people are not going to believe our religious myths.

And you know what? They don't need to. The real shame is that when our brainwashed kids get their pseudo-science debunked at university, they often end up disregarding everything else we taught them. Novelist Anne Rice, in her autobiography, stated that her biggest mistake as a young woman was ending her prayer life with God just because she ended her belief in the Catholic Church. They are not the same thing. There is a difference between our religious beliefs and our relationship with God. The most important thing, in her opinion, is to continue to talk to God regardless of our doubts. The evidence of a loving God is not found in books, services, or religion but in the beauty of nature and human relationships. This, she wrote, is unquestionable.

Jesus once said that the most important thing about faith wasn't proper belief at all but proper love. In fact, he said that if people loved others as he did, the world would begin to believe that he was indeed the Lord of the Universe.

Mess with Santa, but never mess with love. And try not to brainwash your kids.

COPS FOR CANCER

I was late for my radiation therapy in Victoria today, because I got stuck in traffic behind the Cops for Cancer bike-a-thon fundraiser. I was mad. I felt like rolling down my window and shouting at the dozen or so officers on bikes. Can't you see I'm going to be late for my cancer treatment? Then it occurred to me that these cancer-fighting cops probably funded the invention of radiation therapy. So, I gave them a little grace, waited for a break in traffic, and sped past them in the fast lane.

When I finally arrived at the cancer clinic at Royal Jubilee Hospital, I whipped myself down to the radiation wing and spoke quickly to the technician, "Put me in, coach; I'm ready to play."

She quickly changed the table and strapped me in. "Do you want a warm blanket today, Mr. Pankratz?"

"Not today, dear," I responded. "I'm in a hurry, so I'll have to rough it."

Five minutes later, I was done and running to meet my doctor.

"So," my doctor asked, "how are you feeling?"

"Great," I said. "I'm feeling more energetic and better than ever. Are you sure they're doing it right?"

She told me they were indeed radiating my brain properly and according to the right specifications. So, I thanked her and went on my way.

A close friend texted me yesterday expressing his fear about potentially having some kind of heart disease. I guess his heart has been beating irregularly. I felt bad for him, so I texted him to cheer him up: *That's shitty. Let me know what your survival chances are—maybe we can do a joint funeral?*

He texted right back: *Yeah, well, I might go before you.*

Me: *If so, I'll try and rush mine along. I'd hate for you to best me.*

I'm pretty sure he was feeling better after that brief interaction. I do what I can.

My dad and I used to joke about death. He died of pancreatic cancer a couple of years ago. Does my humorous take on death mask my fear or express my hope? Probably a bit of both.

GETTING IT RIGHT

The other night at the pub, one of my regulars brought in a bunch of his friends at around midnight. From a bartender's point of view, this was gold. A bunch of thirsty lads with money to spend? Jackpot. $300 and a nice $50 tip later, they were gone at 1:20 a.m. My favorite moment was when one of the guys came up to me and asked for his fourth double rum and coke.

"I already gave last call," I told him.

"Come on, man," he said, "don't be a bitch."

"Okay," I said, irritatingly, "I might get you the drink, but don't call me a bitch."

"I didn't actually call you a bitch, I just said don't *be* a bitch."

I thought that was pretty intelligent for a young, drunk hillbilly. So, I poured him another double rum and coke.

A while later, he was back, telling me how great I was for keeping the pub open and for allowing them to play some Tupac tunes through the sound system.

Only God can judge me, is that right?
Only God can judge me now
Only God baby, nobody else, nobody else
All you other motherfuckers get out of my business.

Our conversation continued. "Could you be cool and let us smoke some joints in here and hot box the pub? When we're done, we can just wave some air fresheners around."

"Dude," I said, "there are cameras everywhere, and I'd get fired."

"Chill. All you have to say is *I'd totally love to, cuz you guys are fucking awesome, but I just can't cuz of the rules.*"

So that's what I said: "I'd totally love to, cuz you guys are fucking awesome, but I just can't cuz of the rules."

That seemed to satisfy him. As he went back to breakdancing, I scratched my head at how much I still need to learn about the world.

I was visiting an old friend the other day in Victoria, and we were comparing our journeys of leaving evangelical Christianity. He shared how, for many years, he'd tried to fit into the Pentecostal church world and speak in tongues, but it never worked. He felt like he could never get it right. One time, after practicing for hours at home, he went to a church service, proceeded to the front of the sanctuary, and asked the preacher to lay hands on him. Then he recited his memorized tongues speak. The church went nuts. Finally, my buddy was in. Not too long after that, my friend left Christianity. He couldn't fake it anymore. He told me that the moment he left evangelical Christianity, he felt like a burden had been lifted from his shoulders. I joked that his un-conversion story was an inspiring conversion story.

Sometimes people ask me why I stopped being a pastor to become a bartender. Did I lose my faith? I answer that I didn't lose my faith at all. I'm as committed to Jesus today as I've ever been. What I have stopped believing in are the manmade stories from the Bible and any form of manipulative religion. And the anti-gay, anti-women, and anti-love beliefs of evangelical Christianity? I'm done with that stuff, too. It's so freeing to be rid of it. I feel like I've spent over twenty years of my life trying to make the unworkable work.

When I left my last church, a well-meaning individual told me that perhaps a liberal like me would be more comfortable in a United Church than a Baptist Church. So, I tried it. I went to a United Church last Easter. It was easily as boring as most evangelical churches I've ever attended. On top of that, in my opinion, they got Jesus wrong. The meaning of Easter, according to the preacher, is that we need to share more. I kept waiting for her to complete her thought, but that was it. Jesus died to teach us to share. Now, I've read the Bible. I know Jesus died to get forgiveness for everyone, not just to teach us to share. I can learn to share from Barney, the purple dinosaur. I don't need Jesus for that.

I was joking with my Victoria buddy that there appears to be only two types of churches: evangelical churches, where you need to accept the entire Bible as true, have emotional experiences, and be against gays; or liberal churches, where Jesus died to teach us to share. Where's the middle ground? Can't there be a church where Jesus is still the Messiah, offering forgiveness to all, but also where you don't have to be against science, culture, and the marginalized?

I'm not sure about you, but I'm tired of faking it. I'm tired of getting it wrong. And I'm tired of being corrected. Jesus must be bigger than the categories that evangelicals and liberals create. But I'm not strong enough to stay in this middle ground. I feel like the only one. Maybe I'm wrong, and one of the two majorities are right?

In these moments, I try to imagine Jesus coming up to me as I serve at the pub and saying, "Dude, you are so awesome. Please, don't change a thing. Just tell all those other mother-fuckers to get out of your business."

Part Three

SOFT LANDING

He's a new-world man
He's a radio receiver
Tuned to factories and farms
He's a writer and ranger and a young boy bearing arms
He's got a problem with his powers
His weapons on patrol
He's got to walk a fine line
And keep his self-control
Trying to save the day for the old-world man
Trying to pave the way for the third-world man
He's not concerned with yesterday
He knows constant change is here today
He's noble enough to know what's right
But weak enough not to choose it
He's wise enough to win the world
But fool enough to lose it
He's a new-world man
Learning to match the beat of the old-world man
He's learning to catch the heat of the third-world man
He's a new world man

—RUSH

THANK YOU FOR MY LIFE

"How are you doing today, Mr. Pankratz?" the radiation thera-pist asked.

"I'm kicking radiation therapy's ass," I replied, energetically.

"Ha! I'm proud of you," she said.

My hair is thin. I've lost thirty pounds. I'm feeling tired. Gas is expensive. But I'm not going to bitch about all that. I'm still living like a king. Being alive is the second-greatest gift.

My wife is the real soldier. I work at the pub every night, drive to Victoria every morning, and nap every afternoon. But Lana, she works every day in Nanaimo and then takes care of the kids and the house chores every night. She's a warrior. Like Xena. Or Red Sonja. But even better looking. And Red Sonja is damn good looking.

I remember as a kid thinking about my future. I always hoped I'd end up spending my life with a tanned woman with black hair. I was living in monochrome Nanaimo at the time. So, when Lana came into my life, I was like a cat on a cricket. She was my woman and has been ever since.

I dragged this woman of mine to tiny red-necked Crofton almost four years ago. She gave up everything she knew—family, friends, good food, and people like her. I'll never be able to repay her. Is being married easy? Of course not. We almost gave up on this marriage numerous times. But we both feel like we've invested too much time, recovered from too many wounds, and drained too much blood to give up now. No one knows me like Lana. And no one knows her, or ever will know her, like I do. We're doomed to spend our lives together. That makes me happy. No one has seen the worst of me like she has, yet she forgives me and is still in love with me. What else could I ask for?

Forgiveness, of course, is the greatest gift.

I was sitting in my hot tub the other day drinking a very large Purple Pirate. A Purple Pirate is equal parts Captain Morgan's spiced rum and Welch's grape juice. Just imagine pirate communion juice, if the pirate was a Baptist. As I watched the seemingly stationary stars above me zip through space at unfathomable speeds, I began to feel close to God.

"Lord, thank you for my life. I've never heard you speak. I've never seen you do one miracle of healing. I've never spoken in tongues or felt touched by an angel. In fact, I've never seen you show any interest in me or my life. And even though I've never smoked or been an alcoholic, I'm the one who got cancer, and now my family suffers with all kinds of future uncertainty. Damn those early nineties cell phones. But I don't begrudge you any of that. I'm not mad. Because I believe you've forgiven me, and for that I'll be eternally grateful. And I'm sure my family is, and always has been, in good hands. Thank you. Thank you for my life."

Life's too good to bitch about. In this moment at least, I feel free.

POWER WORDS

I learned a new power word in a text message the other day.
I suppose it's two words, but together, they form a metaphor
that, until recently, was unknown to me.

My friend, Morty, texted: *Matt Mei did a version of one of
my songs. It's sooo good.*

Me: *Sweet. On iTunes yet?*

Morty: *No, not yet. We're working on some stuff. But he did a
rough version that shows a shit ton of potential.*

And that's how I learned the power-word combo: "shit
ton." As soon as Lana got home from work, I shared my new
phonetic discovery with her. In her typical fashion, she told
me that she not only knew that power-word combo, she uses
it on a regular basis. Damn.

She immediately gave me two examples:

Lana: *I got a shit ton of registered letters today* and *I had to
deliver a shit ton of parcels.*

It was a bit deflating. It was like telling her I won $10 in
the lottery and having her respond that she'd won $100 in the
lottery today, yesterday, and the day before that.

Then I started looking for a chance to use my new power-
word combo. It didn't take long. I saw my buddy Larry walking
his dog as I rode my bike to work. I wasn't wearing my helmet
that day, just my flat tweed cap, which I use to hide my cancer
baldness. He mentioned that he liked my cap and wanted to
buy one just like it but brown. I told him to go to the Bay in

Victoria, where I got mine. "They have a shit ton of brown caps there," I said. I felt like I'd won $100 in the lottery.

I've always taught our kids that there are no bad words, only powerful ones. So, every so often, I teach them a new power word. For example, Hudson's thick-soled shoes are asskickers, their dad is a badass, etc. I only ask them not to use the power word unless it's absolutely necessary. Dancing around singing about vaginas and penises is not an appropriate use of power words.

One time the kids and I were hiking down a hill on Saltspring Island when Hudson discovered the joy of sliding down the slope instead of hiking down. He was extremely happy, as happy as a kid playing a videogame where you get to blow up Sesame Street characters with TNT. At the bottom of the hill, Hudson asked me a very serious question.

"Dad," he asked, "this was so fun. Can I please use a power word?"

"Sure, Hudson," I replied. "Go for it."

"That was fucking awesome!"

"Yes, it sure was, Hudson. But don't tell your mother that. She already thinks she's better than me."

It's hard to tell if Jesus used power words. He spoke a language called Aramaic, but his biographers took his words and translated them into Greek to reach a larger audience. Greek was the common language of the Roman Empire, so having Jesus speak Greek allowed millions of people to access his ideas and deeds.

In the Greek Bible, Jesus uses some powerful words. He calls his enemies names like "that old fox," "brood of vipers," and "whitewashed tombs." It may sound tame, but in Greek, those are powerful insults. Jesus didn't play well with others.

There are, however, two or three occasions where Jesus' biographers didn't translate his words into Greek but used his actual Aramaic words. One of those times was when Jesus was praying. It's recorded that Jesus referred to God as "Abba." In Aramaic, "Abba" means "Dad." Why would Jesus' biographers leave Abba in their Greek book instead of simply using the Greek translation of "Dad"?

Here's my take on it. Something always gets lost in translation. Jesus' biographers didn't want us to miss this bit. So, they didn't translate what Jesus called God. I am invited to talk to God the same way Jesus did. There's no difference between our importance.

Do I pray to God as Abba? No, that feels silly. To me, Abba is a disco band from Sweden that once encouraged me to take a chance on them. But in the arena of prayer, I have the same closeness to God as the Son of Man did. That idea gives me a shit ton of hope.

DANCING WITH TIBETANS

I used to have a friend who hated birds. He said it was because birds don't have hands. He just couldn't relate to any creature that didn't have hands. He didn't like horses for the same reason. He did like monkeys and apes. And raccoons, of course, because they have hands. This friend also told me that, as a kid, he thought he invented masturbation. That could be why he valued hands so highly.

I've always taught my kids to value people who are different than them. For example, I tell them that Sikhs and indigenous people are warriors. They come from a heritage thick with great achievements and courageous survival. Their history demands our admiration, not our pity—and definitely not our scornful disrespect.

One time Ellie came home and told us she didn't like Chinese people. We were shocked. But after some conversation, we realized she had heard some redneck kid at school say disparaging things about Chinese people. Ellie wanted to see our reaction. We reminded her that many of our dearest Vancouver friends are Chinese. That is the one downside of life in a small monochrome town: not much diversity.

I try though. I have befriended pretty much every non-white person in our town of two thousand or so people. From the Vietnamese girls working at the local market to the one elderly Chinese couple who live down the street to the brown guy who owns the other pub, I know them all. Their friendships keep me culturally sane.

I've travelled a bit in my life. I've made friends with people very different than myself. Ex-guerilla fighters in Nicaragua, Tibetan cowboys in Western China, migrant workers in Mexico, Chinese Muslims in northern China. I have wonderful memories of dancing with communist Han Chinese, drawing in the dirt with Qiang Chinese, and singing with Ha Chinese. The Ha could sing with what seemed like two voices at the same time. It was beautiful. And when Tibetans sing, they put one hand on their cheek in a cup fashion. Apparently, it helps amplify their voice.

When I came back from my first trip to China, I went to visit my grandmother and excitedly told her of all my adventures. Her response was, "So, you danced?"

Mennonites are against dancing. My grandmother was very Mennonite. Her reaction was one part funny and one part sad. (By the way, do you know why Mennonites don't have sex standing up? It might lead to dancing.)

People often ask Lana what her cultural heritage is. I always encourage her not to answer. Usually, people just want to put her in a cultural box. Indian...or Spanish...or Hawaiian? Brown people never ask her. They couldn't give a shit.

I used to have a great picture of Jesus having supper with his twelve disciples. It was in the style of da Vinci's "Last Supper." Except for one major difference: everyone was either black or brown. It was an awesome picture. Closer to the truth than da Vinci's version.

I know it's natural to stick with people with whom you think you can relate best. That's why, in a classroom full of diversity, one often finds the most divisions. I guess I'm just saying that doing what's natural isn't always doing what's best. And if I had to choose between having hands or having wings, I'd choose wings.

TOPPING IT UP

Last Friday, I had my head strapped onto the radiation therapy bed for the last time. "Hey," I said to the radiation technician, "why not give me a little extra today, just to top it up? It's going to be a while before I come back here."

"Mr. Pankratz," she said, "you're never coming back here."

A lot of people have told me, with confidence, that I'll beat this cancer. A woman at the pub the other night, after hearing a bit of my story, stood up and hugged me for ten minutes. Four glasses of white wine and the sight of an adorable guy like me will do that to a girl. "I can read auras," she said. "Your cancer is already gone."

That's nice.

I like nice people. It's sweet of people to attempt to encourage me. Whether it's nurses telling me that radiation therapy has cured me or tipsy huggers offering me healing prayers, aura readings, or even cancer-curing mushrooms, they all mean well and are simply trying to lift my spirits.

When my father was dying of pancreatic cancer, some well-meaning Christians came over to his house to anoint him with oil and pray over him. They were nice people who were honestly trying to do something good. My dad would have no part of it though. He politely refused their healing offer and suggested they just sit, talk, and sing instead.

I bet you didn't know that it hurts when Christians put their hands on your head and shoulders to pray for your healing. As the prayers go on and on, the prayer warriors' arms become tired, and they unconsciously begin pressing harder on your body. Multiply that by the number of people praying, and by the end of the prayer time, you feel like you've been whiplashed in a car accident. You may need to request further prayers—for your compressed spine.

I prefer hugs from tipsy aura readers. Maybe I lack faith. Probably. But what is faith anyway? Andy Stanley defines faith as believing that God will keep his promises. Hope, on the other hand, is wishing God would make more promises. Makes sense to me. When we get faith and hope mixed up, we end up either mad at God for breaking promises he never made, or sad, because we didn't know that God has made some promises to us.

In my high school, a group of roving charismatic Christian teenagers acted like God's gangsters. They would roam around the halls, challenging the 1980s Satanists to fights, tossing gospel tracts out windows, and yelling for other teenagers to repent. They also offered healing prayers to the sick, who had enough faith to be cured. One of my buddies suffered from a disease that was slowly atrophying his muscles. I would often skip class and whisk him out of the school in his wheelchair to have some laughs and look at girls. We had many heated games of Risk together and once took a road trip to Calgary. These charismatic lunatics told my buddy that the reason he was in a wheelchair was because he didn't have enough faith to walk.

Shitheads.

Wanting to walk again isn't about faith; it's about hope. We all wish our lives could get better—better health, better wealth, better relationships, and so on. But God never promised these things. I *hope* my cancer is eradicated. But I don't have faith that it will be. Because God never made that promise to me.

That's why my father refused healing prayers. God never made that promise to him, either. What has God promised us? One of Jesus' friends wrote that Jesus promised grace to everyone in need. Just grace. And mercy, too. That's about it.

There's an ancient short prayer that goes like this: Lord Jesus Christ, Son of God, have mercy on me, a sinner. Sometimes I prefer the even shorter version: God, please, help me.

The dinner special the other day at the pub was shepherd's pie. One customer asked if it was real shepherd's pie.

"Are you asking me if we use real shepherds in the pie?" I replied. "That's not only illegal, it's cannibalism. Or are you asking me if real shepherds come here and order it? I actually have sold two to local sheep herders."

"I just want to know if it tastes good," the customer said, only slightly bemused.

Good communication is all about semantics, the meaning of words. Do I have faith that my cancer will be removed miraculously? No. I've never heard God communicate that promise to me. I've never heard God communicate anything to me. But I do hope.

What do I have faith in? I have faith that grace and mercy are available whenever I need them, because two thousand years ago, some friends of Jesus wrote that it's a promise. And I've experienced it. Every time I've asked God for grace and mercy, I've received both. Sure, it's an invisible product, but I don't care. I need it.

And in two weeks, when I begin three types of chemotherapy, lasting over thirty-six weeks, I'll be asking God to give me a little extra grace and mercy that day, just to top me up.

THE INDIFFERENCE OF GOOD MEN

The other day at the pub, a hammered sixty-two-year-old customer was trying to convince me not to cut him off.

"Dude," I said, "you're tottering like an old tree in a windstorm. I'm afraid you're going to fall over. I can't serve you."

"Do you know what I did for twenty-five years, smartass?" the faller proclaimed. "I worked in the woods as a faller! Now give me another drink!"

I guess he didn't recognize how unconvincing that was: I won't fall down, because I was a faller. In his mind, I should have been instantly persuaded. But then he did something that did convince me he could handle a few more St. Remys. Like Frosty, he began to dance around. And he had some seriously gnarly moves for a sixty-two-year-old former faller.

"Alright, you sober young sapling," I said as I poured him a double, "bottoms up!"

There's a scene from the movie *Boondock Saints* where a Catholic priest challenges his congregation to get more involved in the lives of vulnerable people. "We must all fear evil men," he says, "but there is another kind of evil which we must fear most, and that is the indifference of good men."

The worst thing about the Christian movement, as I've experienced it, is the lack of interest church people have in those who don't attend their churches. Not only do few Christian people pay attention to the poor, vulnerable, and abused around the world, but they pay even less attention to the spiritual emptiness that plagues their own communities. And they have lots of excuses for why they don't tell people about God's message of forgiveness.

Church Person #1: I don't talk about Jesus, because I don't want to offend anyone.

Church Person #2: I don't talk about Jesus, because I don't know how.

Church Person #3: I don't talk about Jesus, because I don't have any unchurched friends.

The truth is, they just don't care enough to figure out how to share with their friends and family the thing that they say means the most to them: the freedom that comes from being forgiven. The truth is, they are indifferent to the spiritual emptiness of good people. It gets worse. The few Christians who do try and tell others about God tend to butcher the story of Jesus. Like mixing a shitty cocktail, they add too much to the simple story of Jesus.

They add fucked-up science: Don't you know evolution is a hoax?

They add fucked-up politics: If you vote liberal, you're pro-abortion.

They add fucked-up social policy: But the Bible condemns homosexuality!

Then they remove a tasty dose of reality and forget to put in the double shot of imagination.

The result is an undrinkable concoction.

Please, don't hear me wrong. The people trying to convince others about Jesus mean well—most of the time. But they have added this strange evangelical (or Catholic or Orthodox) culture to the simple message that forgiveness is free.

One of my biggest challenges when I was a Young Life missionary to high school kids in East Vancouver was motivating the kids to attend church. Many youth loved our clubs, camps, and Bible study groups. They received hope in their hearts as we loved them and shared the simple message that forgiveness is free and following Jesus is meaningful.

But when we attempted to transition them to church, church attendance rarely stuck. The few kids who tried entering church buildings felt awkward and unworthy. They didn't dress right, act right, or believe right. Besides that, church services are too early in the morning. Few kept going. They wanted spiritual freedom but ended up feeling like they had to adopt a restrictive alien culture.

One of my biggest regrets from that period was when a young man came to me during a camping trip and told me that he wanted to experience forgiveness and follow Jesus' ways.

"That's great," I responded, "now you also have to stop smoking pot and having sex before marriage."

Suddenly, what was exciting for him became a burden. By denying him his two favorite pastimes, I was trying to get him to drink water mixed with horseshit. The ironic thing is that I had sex before I was married. And I just ate a medicinal pot brownie prior to writing this.

Jesus once compared believers who don't share the hope of God to unfruitful plants whose roots don't go very deep. He said the worries of this world and the deceitfulness of riches will keep lots of believers from being fruitful. In other words, selfishness and the desire for more things keeps believers mute. The indifference of good men.

Leslie Newbigin once said that the Church is the only organization that exists for the needs of non-members. Our primary focus isn't supposed to be teaching our kids to believe in an infallible Bible, raising enough money to pay our pastor, or creating a closer spiritual family by having more potluck lunches. Our primary focus is supposed to be doing whatever it takes to share hope with spiritually thirsty people.

That means finding new ways to convince a skeptical world that our greatest need has finally been met, our need for forgiveness. Learning a new dance can be difficult, but once you figure it out, people will want to watch your gnarly moves. And because I don't know any churches trying to learn this dance, I still don't go.

THE KILLER BEES

This has been a painful two days. Yesterday, the dentist jabbed four long needles into my lower left gum to extract an abscessed tooth. Then it got worse. He reached for the vice-grips. As the dentist wiggled the rotten tooth, we realized the area wasn't frozen yet. Fireworks. So, they inserted three more needles. Vice-grips. Fireworks. Then three more needles. Vice-grips. When my mouth went wild again, the dentist told me I had what they call a live nerve—unwilling to be sedated. Eventually, they gave up, and I left with my mouth hurting like a son of a gun. Ten needles will do that. This Friday, I'll be going back to receive a much stronger intravenous anesthesia to have the bad tooth extracted. It has to come out before chemo starts in two weeks. Chemo hits the immune system—hard. My immune system has to heal up from the tooth surgery before my first chemo injection.

I bought a plot of land near the ocean the other day and plan to build a spec house on it. I'm not getting rich working at the pub for nine bucks an hour. Today, with my sore mouth, I rented a hedge trimmer from Home Depot to begin tackling the overgrown hedges on the property. It was either that or fall asleep at home. You see, I'm tired most of the time. Apparently, by keeping busy, I'll be healthier. Something about adrenaline being better than bed rest. So, I decided to try and keep busy with power tools. I was making great headway, too.

Until I woke up a wasp nest. I dropped the hedge trimmer and bolted. Maybe I should have just napped after all.

Neighborhood Ninja is building the investment house with me. As I've mentioned before, he is not only a friend and a builder but also a legitimate ninja. In fact, he trained in Japan with the last verified ninja in the world. You'd never suspect him to be a secret assassin, and that's probably why he's so good at it. He's all smiles and giggles—until the ninja stars and katana swords come out. I try and stay on his good side.

He's been on my case to apply for a Homeowners Protection Policy for this new house we're building. I've tried to make the appropriate calls and visit the appropriate websites, but I can't figure out how to get this important document. So, he did it himself. In five minutes. I texted him my thanks: *Dude, you know how to get shit done. I try my hardest, and I just get stung by bees.*

Neighborhood Ninja: *You're bee-ing hilarious.*

The dentist office where I'll be sedated on Friday is the office of a Doctor Miner. I went in to make my appointment with the rather dour-looking receptionist.

"Is this the right office for Doctor Miner?" I asked.

"Yes," the dour receptionist said. "Is there something I can help you with?"

"Does that mean he has two jobs?"

Pause. Awkward laughter. I thought that was comedic gold. She thought it was fool's gold.

Some customers pick on me at work, because I'm a Christian and a former pastor. One drunk customer told me that he can't stand Christians.

Kid Cook stood up for me. "Christians are fine," he said. "It's Jehovah's Witnesses I can't stand. Jehovah's Witnesses come to your door, but you have to go to the Christians' door."

Good point, in a back-handed, ironic kind of way.

I have a bunch of medicinal cannabis products that I've never used. I'm just too busy to get stoned. I was hoping that medicinal marijuana would give me energy. Not so. One time I tried the concentrated stuff, and I could barely get my kids to school in the morning. I couldn't feel my legs. I was dragging myself around like a cat with a spinal infection. I hate feeling baked.

As I soaked in my hot tub tonight and drank Captain Morgan's spiced rum straight out of the bottle (because I'm out of grape juice), I couldn't stop rubbing my itchy wasp-stung arm. My forearm has swelled up like Popeye's after eating spinach. Yes, I had only gotten stung once, but it was a bitch.

I thought to myself, what is pain? Some of us run from it, some of us complain about it, and some of us insure ourselves against it. Me? I talk to it. It's something I learned from Kid Cook.

Feel pain? Fuck you, pain.

Feel sad? Fuck you, sadness.

Got an incurable illness? Fuck you, illness.

Get stung by wasps? Fuck you, wasps.

Chuck Palahniuk, the author of one of my favorite books-turned-movies, *Fight Club*, once wrote about pain: "It's so hard to forget pain, but it's even harder to remember sweetness. We have no scar to show for happiness. We learn so little from peace."

That is bang on. So, instead of focusing on my pain, I'll end this chapter with thankfulness.

Thank you, Neighborhood Ninja. Thank you, Bar Guy. Thank you, Doctor Miner. Thank you, Chuck Palahniuk. And thank you, Captain Morgan.

(NOT) PRAYING FOR CHECKERS

We're short-staffed at the pub, so I've been working six nights a week. The other day, I came home from work at 1 a.m. and found a note from Ellie: "I love you Daddy so much. I wish you could stay home with us. I wish the money just came by itself. Xoxoxoxoxoxoxoxoxoxo"

Our cat, Checkers, didn't stay home with us either. Nor did he come back by himself. He just up and disappeared. As each week passed, I thought it was more and more likely that he'd gotten his friendly self into the belly of a local bear or cougar. Or perhaps the angry neighbor down the street had poisoned Checkers and buried him in his yard. Lana worked her ass off trying to get Checkers back. She put up posters. She contacted every local vet and animal shelter. She even went door-to-door canvassing for that stupid cat.

I didn't pray for Checkers to come home. Not because I don't like him; I do. I'm just not convinced that prayer makes a difference. I don't pray for my cancer. I didn't pray for my tooth-extraction pain, though I did thank God for the postoperative Valium high. I don't even pray for the drunks at the bar to sober up and find Jesus. If God answered that prayer, I'd be looking for a new job.

I was arguing with some Christian patrons at the pub the other night about the merits of praying for pets. They were trying to persuade me that since God cares about sparrows and birds, he also cares about pets. Smartass that I am, I brought up one of my favorite things that Jesus once said: "Don't bother praying for stuff because your Heavenly Father already knows what you need. He'll take care of the world with or without your prayers."

I remember an unbelieving kid who came to an evangelistic camp on Thetis Island (we called it Fetus Island) I was running years ago. One of the exercises we made the kids do on the second-to-last night was to go out by themselves and talk to God. So, the skeptical kid went down to the dock by the ocean to pray: "God, if you're real, please make a cow swim out of the ocean and come up to me on this dock. I'll hop on the cow and ride it back to mug-up to show Brian that you're real. If you do this, I'll believe and serve you forever."

Last night a young couple came to the pub to eat just before the kitchen was closing. The woman was very hungry. She explained that she was a dance instructor and had just been at a fundraiser for cancer research. It involved two hours of Zumba dancing. As I served her a poutine and an appy platter for two, which she ate all by herself, I told her that I'm fighting cancer. I told her about the new cancer treatment that is shrinking my tumor. I also told her about another treatment coming out of the University of Calgary that is going to add years to the lives of people with fast-growing brain cancer. Then I thanked her for Zumba dancing for cancer research. Her Zumba dancing may have just saved my life.

I see a lot of broken people at the pub. I see a lot of broken people in my neighborhood. I see a lot of broken people at the playground, where my kids go to school. I see a lot of brokenness inside myself. Do you know what restores a bit of that brokenness? Acceptance. Acceptance and love. I think that's why drunk people are so touchy and huggy. They've cast off their protective shell and are instinctively reaching out for someone…anyone…anything…to help them feel a little more whole, a little less broken.

The other day, we received a phone call from our vet telling us that a cat matching Checkers' description had been found near the high school in Chemainus. This was a full five weeks after his sudden disappearance. If the cat was indeed Checkers, that would mean he had left Crofton, crossed the Chemainus River, and trekked over five kilometers, deep into the hinterlands of the City of Murals. Lana called the nice, conscientious woman who had been feeding the cat and asked if it had a tattoo of a mouse in its ear. It did. Lana began to cry on the phone. She hadn't been the same person since Checkers went missing. I'm convinced she loves that cat more than she loves me. Apparently, I'm just not as soft or as easy to get along with. So, Lana went out and brought back our cat—a much lighter, dirtier, and mangier version of Checkers but Checkers nonetheless.

Hudson's first reaction to Checkers' return was less than enthusiastic. He wanted to know if the return of Checkers meant we were no longer going to get a new kitten. I must admit, I was partly to blame for that response. I had already begun making plans to get a new cat. Can you imagine how pissed off and hurt Checkers would have been if I had?

"You motherfuckers replaced me already? It's only been thirty-five days!"

Tonight, I prayed with my kids, like we do most nights when I'm not working, which is about once a week. We prayed that God would bless Mommy, Hudson, and Ellie. We prayed that God would bless Ellie's biological brother, who is on the adoption wait list in Vancouver. We prayed for Ellie's biological mother, father, aunt, and grandmother…that God would bless them all. And we thanked God for bringing Checkers back, even though Daddy didn't pray for him.

Last night in my hot tub, as I was pondering life, I prayed that God would bless my co-workers and those who visit me at the pub. I want God to bless everyone I know. I want them all to know that God has accepted them—whether they want him to or not. I wish everyone I know was happier. Even those I don't know.

I wish money would just come in. I'd like to be at home more. I wish praying about lost pets made them come home. I didn't like having a sad wife for five weeks. I wish praying for sick people made them healthier. Hearing stories of terminally ill kids is heart-wrenching. But I don't really believe in prayer. Even though I do it sometimes. I just can't stop myself.

And in case you were wondering, no cow surfaced out of the ocean that night on Fetus Island, but we had a hilarious time laughing about it over mug-up before bed.

THE UNDERWEAR LIE

We have a rule in our family: no lying. It's the cardinal rule. If you tell the truth, you won't get into trouble, no matter what you've done. I read about this being a very effective parenting strategy in a great book called *Nurture Shock*. The funny thing is, my kids still lie. Hudson's regular lie is about underwear. He hates wearing it. This morning, it happened again.

"So," I asked Hudson, "you dressed?"

"Yes, Dad," he replied confidently.

"*All* dressed?"

"You bet I am, Daddy."

"Tell me the truth, Cub," I said. "You won't get into trouble."

"That is the truth, Dad. I swear on my young life."

"You know it's going to cost you twenty dollars if you're lying," I reminded him.

"I know, Dad," he said sweetly. "Why would I lie to you?"

"Okay then," I said, wanting this to be true, "show me the edge. Pull up the edge."

"Okay, Dad," he said ever so hesitantly. "Here it is."

"Ha! That's not the edge. That's the stretchy belt they put in the waistband of kids' pants!"

"Okay, Dad," he said with a grin, "you got me. I'm lying."

"Go get dressed, you little turd," I said playfully. "And by the way, thanks for the new 3D movie I'm going to buy later at Walmart with your twenty dollars."

"I don't mind, Dad. I wanted you to get you a new movie anyway."

I'm convinced that Lana lies to herself and believes those lies.

I want to use your vape tonight, she texted recently. *Where do you keep the good stuff from the doctor?*

Me: *In the fridge.*

Lana: *Never mind. Your sister just drove up when I pulled it out.*

Me: *Did she see it?*

Lana: *I don't think so. She just dropped off a frozen meal.*

Me: *Perfect for when you get the munchies after.*

Lana: *Munchies? From what?*

Me: *From the vape silly.*

Lana: *You bought a vape?*

Neighborhood Ninja has been doing some renovations on our rental suite next door. As he pulled nails out of the crown molding, we talked about people who believe the lies they tell themselves. He told me that Ninjitsu teaches that when we can accept the fact that we lie to ourselves on a regular basis, we're that much closer to becoming fully realized human beings. I agreed with him. I call it smothering the bad seed. Accepting the truth about yourself and being courageous enough to let others see the real you is the shortest path to free living. And yes, it can be a scary path. We all want people to believe we are the people we wish we were, not the people we know we are.

I was chatting with another friend at the bar last night and comparing ages to see who was older. I was. It was strange that I was surprised. It's not that my friend looks old. It's just that in my mind's eye, I look twelve years old, and to my actual eyes, she looks like a mature woman. In my heart, I still feel like that awkward, immature twelve-year-old boy I was twenty-two years ago. Okay, that was a lie. I was twelve years old thirty-two years ago. I shock myself every time I look in the mirror and see this middle-aged man. It's hard to accept the truth about myself.

There's a scene in the awesome movie *Edge of Tomorrow* (thanks again, Hudson), where Tom Cruise's character, Cage, is attempting to get to know Rita, played by Emily Blunt. She refuses to open up and talk about herself.

"I don't need to get to know you," Rita explains to Cage. "And if you knew what was good for you, you wouldn't want to get to know me either. It's the only way you make it through this thing."

That's how a lot of us live. We lie to ourselves and hide the truth about ourselves from those around us. Maybe we believe it's the only way to get through this thing. I disagree.

I was sitting in my hot tub last night after work thinking about when I started writing this book a few months ago. It was my way of dealing with cancer and leaving evangelical Christianity to become a bartender. I didn't know what would happen if people actually read my writings. But I didn't care. I had to describe for myself, and for my kids when they get older, what was really going on in my head, heart, and soul. I wanted to be real to myself and to those who could handle this new me.

Hammy, a friend of mine, wrote to me about how he's enjoying reading my blog: "So, I've been reading your blog and feeling very uplifted by what you're writing about. It really has been resonating with me. I'm grateful for your voice. You remind people that God's love is bigger than the limits of our imagination. I was weary of the get-out-of-hell-free card evangelism of my youth, because I saw it as conniving and misguided. It's tough being quiet about this stuff."

It's tough telling the truth about ourselves, but it's equally tough keeping the truth about ourselves hidden from others and from ourselves. Might as well tell the truth, I suppose. Even if you get in trouble for it.

SNACKS AND BALLS

I learned a new power word the other day from a regular at the pub named Tequila Sheila. The word is "balls." It was used in a sentence just prior to the pub's Halloween party. Some customers and I were listening to Galaxies Greatest Hits on the pub music system, and a shitty Mariah Carey song came on. I find it hard to believe that "Dreamlover" is a hit around the entire galaxy, but hell, what do I know about the dreams of alien lovers? Midway through the song, Tequila Sheila made an announcement to the entire pub.

"This song is balls!" she exclaimed.

I offered to change it, guessing that if a song was balls, it probably wasn't pleasant for her to listen to. I was right. I changed the music channel to Galaxies Classic Rock. I think the song playing was "New World Man" by Rush. I can't stand Rush, but I'm just the server, and Sheila was the paying customer.

"Oh, great," I said under my breath. "Rush. Rush is balls."

Here's another example of using the word "balls" appropriately: Lana wanted the house to herself Sunday morning, so she could study her mediation textbooks without conflict in the house. I thought (but didn't say) that was ironic. So, I offered to take the kids to church in Duncan. I was under the impression there was a special service happening at Happy Baptist Church in honor of their new lead pastor. I also thought there would be snacks. When the kids and I arrived for the 11 a.m. service, we couldn't find any snacks. Apparently, the snacks would be served the following Sunday. So, I texted Lana.

Me: *Balls. No snacks.*

Lana: *balls!!!!!!! hungry family ;(*

Me: *It's next week. balls. What's Ashley's dad's name? I just saw him at church*

Lana: *Oh my goodness Umm no idea. Bill? lol*

Me: *Doug? Fred?...Dale?*

Lana: *Yes Dale!*

Me: *I'm hungry. Want to buy us pizza?*

Lana: *Sure bring me home a slice*

Me: *Okay*

Lana: *Don't forget to get a cassette tape recorder from the thrift store for Ellie's singing classes.*

Me: *I looked there already. They didn't have any that worked. all shit and balls.*

Maybe you're wondering why I attended a church service considering I've written three chapters about why I *don't* go to church. Three reasons:

1. I'm good with contradictions.

2. I'd rather be part of the solution than the problem.

3. Snacks.

Oh, and a fourth reason: apparently, I needed a nap.

There's even a fifth reason I enjoy church: I like having the communion meal. That's when a person eats a small piece of cracker and drinks grape juice out of a tiny plastic cup. It reminds us of Jesus' body being broken on a cross, like a broken cracker, and Jesus' blood pouring out, like the grape juice being poured into the tiny plastic cup. The preacher asked us to come up to the front of the church, collect our crackers and mouse-sized glasses of virgin Purple Pirate, and return to our seats. We were instructed to wait until everyone had sat down with their mini-meal, so we could eat and drink together. Then he asked us to do one more thing: "Search your heart. Is there anything between you and the Lord? If not, please partake of the communion meal."

So, I did. I found nothing in my heart separating me from the Lord. Then I savored my cracker and pounded down the very unfermented juice.

When I was a professional Christian pastor, I used to include some stand-up comedy in my sermons. I figured a bit of levity would help people stay awake during my messages. But I did get criticized by some parishioners. I shared this experience with Kid Cook.

"I don't understand why anyone would criticize a preacher for trying to be more entertaining," he asked.

"Some people don't listen to sermons to laugh," I explained. "They listen to sermons to feel guilty. It's not a good message if they don't go home feeling like shit."

Joyce Meyer once said that we weren't built for guilt. I like that. Don't get me wrong; sometimes guilt is rational and has a purpose. We need to listen to that feeling and make amends or change a destructive behavior. But a lot of our guilt is irrational and emotional and serves no purpose. Rather than being instructive, false guilt results in sleepless nights, drug dependence, and moodiness. It wrecks people.

Apparently, when Jesus died, a giant curtain that hung in the Jewish temple separating God's presence from regular people was torn in half, symbolizing that our guilt no longer separates us from God's love and acceptance. There is no historical evidence that this event happened, but I like the idea of it, the idea that God could not be closer to me than he is right now. I find this idea liberating. It doesn't always feel true, but when I choose to believe that God accepts me as I am, I seem to stand up taller and care less about the things people say to bring me down. Most of what the haters say is balls anyway.

Part Four

SPACE WALK

There's a voice that keeps on calling me

Down the road, that's where I'll always be.

Every stop I make, I make a new friend,

Can't stay for long, just turn around and I'm gone again

Maybe tomorrow, I'll want to settle down,

Until tomorrow, I'll just keep moving on.

-THE LITTLEST HOBO THEME SONG

THE SMARTWATCH OF
CHRISTMAS PAST

A year and a half ago, I participated in something called crowd-funding. That's when regular people fund a small-business start-up through a website like Indiegogo. The start-up I helped fund was Kreyos Smartwatch. I sent in $250 and was promised two Dick Tracy-style wristwatch phones that would work in tandem with the iPhone 4. I thought it would be a great gift for Lana and me for last Christmas.

It's almost Christmas again, and the Star Trek watches still haven't arrived. Lana keeps asking me when her Christmas present for last year will arrive, and I keep telling her: "It's in the mail."

Kreyos started out as a company asking for $100,000 in start-up money to produce the only smartwatch with voice and gesture control. They surpassed expectations and eventually raised over $1.5 million from early adopting rubes like me. In my research today, I discovered that one of the Kreyos founders, Steve Tan, was recently spotted in a brand-new Ferrari and that there is a Facebook campaign of angry backers like myself demanding a full refund. The initial four thousand backers actually received watches, but they were fraught with problems. The rest of us who signed up later have received jack shit.

In other words, I will probably not receive anything for my $250 investment other than the knowledge that I helped

Steve Tan get a new Ferrari. I hope you like your Ferrari, Steve. You're not welcome.

A great band, called the Headless Betties, was playing at the pub's Halloween party last Friday. They reminded me of a female-led Mumford and Sons. The lead singer of the Headless Betties was dressed up like a mime. She was a shitty mime but a fantastic singer. They did a great cover of Edward Sharpe and the Magnetic Zeros hit song, "Home."

> *Well, hot and heavy pumpkin pie*
> *Chocolate, candy, Jesus Christ*
> *Ain't nothing please me more than you*
> *Home, let me come home*
> *Home is wherever I'm with you.*

I've been reading a book called *Jesus Interrupted* by Bart Ehrman. Bart's goal in the book is to share with regular folk like me what most biblical scholars have known for years: the Bible is fraught with problems. There are internal contradictions, historical inaccuracies, and disagreements between the writers. That said, Bart also writes that many of these biblical scholars still have faith. Bart himself is an agnostic, but not because of the problems in the Bible. He's an agnostic, because he can't square the idea of a loving God with the reality of pain and suffering in the world.

One example of the problems in the Bible is John, the writer of five New Testament books. Apparently, he changed the story of the historical Jesus, adding bits from his own ideas and erasing bits from other writers he didn't like. His gospel, the Gospel of John, is significantly different from the gospels of Matthew, Mark, and Luke—to the point of being contradictory at times. Does this bother me? Not so much. Here's something John once wrote that begins to show why: "We declare to you what was from the beginning, what we have heard, what we have seen, what we have looked at and touched with our hands, this is the message - that we should love one another."

John is asking me to trust the truth about the priority of love. Why? Because he says he was with Jesus. They used to wrestle around the campfire. And within his letters and gospels are buried some of the real teachings of the historical Jesus. And what's the most important teaching of Jesus? Yeah, it's love.

It doesn't bother me that Steve Tan bought a new Ferrari with my $250. He may still send me a smartwatch. And if he doesn't, I learned a $250 lesson.

It doesn't bother me that the lead singer of the Headless Betties is a better singer than she is a mime. And it doesn't bother me that some of the stuff John wrote is bullshit. Because some of it *isn't* bullshit.

The only thing that bothers me is what Lana's going to say when she reads this chapter and discovers the truth about her Christmas present.

Postscript - The Day After

I should note that Steve Tan wrote a nice apology letter back in August claiming he never bought a new car with any of the funding money. If you'd like to read it, just google "Steve Tan," "Ferrari," and "I don't have a clue how to make a smartwatch."

Steve, if you're reading this, I'm sorry for that last bit. I look forward to finally getting my smart watches soon. Trust me when I tell you that my overreaching hubris and I have made a shit ton of mistakes in our lives, too. And don't worry about those threatening letters from my wife. I heard those same words when she read this chapter yesterday. Hopefully, she'll forgive us both by Christmas. In the meantime, can I crash at your place?

SALMON PORN

Apparently, last week I signed up to chaperone Hudson's class of nine-year-olds to the Nanaimo Fish Hatchery. I didn't remember signing up. When Hudson reminded me of my obligation, I told him that I was hoping to nap today.

"Well, Dad," he said, "I guess that's not going to happen."

It reminded me of the time this past summer when I was showing off on Hudson's little BMX bike and turned too sharp on its under-inflated tires, resulting in me sprawled out bleeding all over the street.

"Well, Dad," he said, "I guess you learned a lesson."

"You little shit," I blurted, "now help me get up and pick the rock shards out of my face and hands."

I texted Lana after Hudson informed me that I would not be napping this morning: *I don't remember signing up for a field trip.*

Lana: *Um, you didn't. But we did sign him up to go.*

Me: *Well, I'm going to go anyway. I'm going to trip the shit out of this field trip.*

Lana: *Awe, I love u. Got my flu shot.*

Me: *Nice one. We're getting ours today after school. Oh, Hudson says good job mom.*

Lana: *Awe thanks!*

Me: *He never says good job to me. You <u>should</u> be thankful.*

Underlines added for effect. Apparently, you can't text underlines. Technology is balls.

Because my chemotherapy is starting next week, my oncologist requires me and everyone in my house to get a flu shot. Chemotherapy is effective at killing cancer cells, because cancer cells tend to divide rapidly. So do white blood cells. As a result, my infection-fighting white blood cells will get the shit kicked out of them during chemotherapy. To try and counter this reality, it's important for me to keep far away from germs. In fact, I was told at chemo school the other day that if I ever get a fever above 37.5°C, I'm to rush myself to Duncan Emergency.

Ellie was terrified to get her flu shot after school today but still said she'd do it. I warned her in the car on the way to the clinic that I'd have to hold her down if she changed her mind at the doctor's office. She promised me that she'd be strong and get her shot without complaining. But once the nurse arrived in our clinic room with the child-sized needle, she broke down.

"Daddy," she pleaded, "please don't let her do it. Please, please. I don't want to get a flu shot anymore. I love you. Please make her stop, Daddy. Please!"

"Hurry, nurse!" I whispered, with Ellie in a headlock. "I won't be able to hold her down much longer."

Nature, as I've said before, is a mean and surly bitch. Salmon reproduction is a prime example. The nature lady at the hatchery explained to us how salmon spawn. Each spawning female lays about 2,500 eggs. Of those eggs, only two or three return from their ocean adventures to the place of their birth to spawn. The other 2,498 or so salmon die, either as eggs, as fry, or as adult salmon. The two or three salmon who are lucky enough to return to their spawning grounds finally get to have some well-deserved sex.

Mommy Salmon: "I've just survived attacks from killer whales and indigenous harvesters. I've swam up this shallow river, scraping my underbelly on the rocks and my top side on tree branches. I look like shit. I feel like shit. I'll just roll over here on these rocks, release my eggs, and die. Hopefully, some male salmon will come by and fertilize them within sixty seconds, before all the eggs become inert and useless. Good night, cruel world. Out you go, my sweet eggs. Ahhhhhhhh..."

Daddy Salmon: "Oh, look over there, it's a sexy female salmon about to lay her eggs. She's definitely weathered, but like the song suggests, 'If you can't be with the one you love, honey, love the one you're with.' Oh shit, she just died. Now to let this milt out...ahhhhhhhhh...I need a cigarette."

After the nature lady's explanation of salmon reproduction, I leaned over to one of the other chaperones and whispered an aside, "Sure takes the fun out of sex."

"No kidding," she replied. "Makes me want to rush home and watch some salmon porn on the internet."

Actually, I said both of those comments to the other chaperone. She just laughed hysterically. Or it could have been awkwardly....

Salmon reproduction also occurs another way. The workers at the hatchery take a female salmon, kill her with a quick blow to the head from a wooden club, slit her stomach open, and release her eggs into a bucket being held by a nine-year-old girl. Then they take a male salmon and rub his belly, causing him to release his milt into a cup being held by a nine-year-old boy, which is then used to fertilize the eggs. The male salmon is released and dies approximately two days later. The nine-year-olds watching this live demonstration thought it was the greatest thing since that guy recorded "Gangnam Style."

I felt sick. I don't remember going on field trips like that when I was a kid. I just remember feeding bread crumbs to ducks. Again, I wondered if I should have just stayed home and napped.

The kid who works in the liquor store came up to me the other day at the pub, in front of the other staff, and announced that he had come up with a new nickname for me.

"Brian," he teased, "I've thought of a new nickname for you because of your bald head: Baby Huey."

"Well," I said, not wanting to be outdone, "I've thought of a new nickname for you, too: Who's Baby Huey?"

I read recently that I'm destined to remain bald. Hair that falls out during chemotherapy grows back, often thicker than before, but hair that falls out during radiation therapy, like mine did, will probably never grow back, except in patches. That's why I'm sporting my much-maligned mini-Mohawk. I tell people I do what I can with what I've got. It's like reverse balding—hair on top but nothing around the crown. I was rubbing my bald spots this evening and thinking about cancer and death. I know that radiation therapy and chemotherapy aren't cures. They're just ways to buy time. Because of these experiences, every day and every year I have left is special. So is every day, and every year we all have left.

I have to believe this life isn't the end. Death must be a rebirth—a beginning, not an ending. There must be more to this life than struggling up a shallow river only to have some sex, birth some kids, and die. Unlike the fish hatchery lady, knowing that my dead body will give food to bears and trees isn't enough for me. There must be more.

Sitting in my hot tub tonight, I thought about whether this life is all there is. Jesus believed there was more. Apparently, he said that when we die, we'll be with him in paradise. It freaks me out a little that the people who recorded Jesus saying these words may have made them up. Since leaving the evangelical Christian faith I grew up with, I've really missed the certainty of my former beliefs. I loved my certainty. Now

I have way more doubts and fears. I suppose I'm a lot like most people now.

Maybe faith burns brightest when doubts are the strongest, because for faith to be real, it must not stop swimming up the raging fish ladder of uncertainty. After all, without uncertainty, there would be no need for faith, right?

One of my favorite Bible verses is Matthew 28:17. It says that after Jesus rose from the dead, he climbed a mountain with his friends to ascend to heaven. Prior to Jesus' ascension, this group of followers worshiped him on that mountain. It says that when they saw him, they worshiped him—but some of them doubted.

Then Jesus zoomed into heaven.

It's one of my favorite verses, because in it, God seemed okay with their worship and with their doubt. I hope he's okay with mine.

On the day I die, and probably cry my way into the next life, I have faith it will be more like being held in a loving headlock then receiving a quick blow to the head with a wooden club.

I also have faith that when Hudson eventually arrives to join me there, many years later, he'll finally say, (underline added for effect), "_Good job, Dad_."

FREE BIRD

Lana and I had a little conflict the other day that stirred up a disproportionate amount of anger in me, resulting in the cancellation of my cell-phone plan and the deactivation of my Facebook account. I wanted to be left alone.

The argument? She thinks I should stop drinking two weeks prior to the start of chemotherapy. I think I should stop drinking two *days* prior to the start of chemotherapy. I keep telling her that if she just had a drink with me, she'd see it my way. The apple wine I made from abandoned orchard apples is that good. I think it's even cancer-fighting.

When Lana asked me why I cancelled my cell phone and Facebook account, I told her it had little to do with our argument. This anger has been building up in me for a long while now. Our little conflict just brought it out. What is causing this anger? It could be the string of ministry failures over the past twenty-five years. It could be the death of my father. It could be the unending challenges of married life and parenthood. It could be the feeling of being abandoned by church people, by God, by my health. Who knows?

Regardless, I found myself sending a final text to Lana when she asked why I've buried myself in a metaphorical luddite cave and unfriended my 675 closest buddies.

Me: *I just want everyone to fuck off and leave me alone. Including God. Oh, and Jesus, too.*

Lana: *You unfriended Jesus? I didn't even know he had a Facebook account.*

Here are three people who made me mad today:

1. The neighbor woman, who told me to stop trimming my hedges on my empty lot with a rented chainsaw, because I was disturbing a family of hummingbirds. I told her I had a meeting with the hummingbirds earlier that morning, and they were fine with the work I was doing. She didn't think that was funny.

2. The nice guy who helped me fix the chainsaw I rented to trim my hedges on my empty lot, because he kept quoting Bible verses. Not at me, just in general. It pissed me off. I told him that the Bible was full of myths and legends just to get him to stop. He thought that was funny.

3. The old guy who was impatiently waiting at the rental place where I rented the shitty chainsaw that kept breaking as I was trimming my hedges. He wanted to rent some scaffolding and was telling the attendant to hurry up. His impatience made me mad. I asked the attendant if old people shouldn't be more patient. I mean, they've had sixty-plus years to figure out the world hasn't worked, nor will it ever work, according to their schedule. Or does their sense of entitlement just grow bigger as the years pass?

I'm entitled to my anger, because I get mad about important things, like Bible-quoting Christians and hummingbird-loving neighbors.

Tonight at the pub, the faller was hitting on a girl forty years younger than him. After his seventh attempt to tell her how cute she was and ask her if she wanted to let her hair down from the toque she was wearing and dance, I lost it. As I stepped in front of the old man as he made his final attempt at a Last Tango in Paris, he grabbed my hand for a handshake to express our continued friendship. He knew I had the power to ban him from the pub. As he held my hand in a firm grip, I felt the anger rising in me again.

"Old faller," I said sternly, "you're starting to make me very angry. Leave that girl alone. She's not interested in dancing or even talking with you. This is my bar, and if you don't listen to me, I will toss you out of here like a motherfucking...gnat."

(I couldn't think of anything better than "gnat" at the time.)

"But—"

"I don't care if you've been a faller for twenty-five years, in the Navy for five years, and went to Saigon in nineteen seventy-one. And please let go of my hand; you're hurting me. This drunken handshake is over."

"Are we still friends and shit?" the faller asked.

"Yes, we're still friends and shit."

As the night wore on, it became very quiet, as the faller was now the only person in the bar.

"Do you know what the difference between you and me is?" he asked. "I have charisma. In the seventies, I was getting laid, smoking pot, popping amphetamines...those were the best years of my life. Do you know that young girl I was talking to?"

"You mean the one who snuck out the back door, so you wouldn't see her?"

"She'll be back," he said confidently. "She'll be coming home with me tonight."

"No, she won't, man. She's not coming back."

"I bet you five thousand dollars she'll be back in fifteen minutes."

I shook my head confidently. "Won't happen, man."

Fifteen minutes later, and five thousand dollars poorer, the faller was tearful.

"Can you call me a taxi?" he asked.

"I'll drive you home, buddy," I offered gently. "I'm off in twenty minutes. You live in a trailer in the mobile home park, right?"

"Yeah," the faller said sadly. "I miss the seventies. I was hot shit in the seventies, man."

I used to believe that anything good I did in life wasn't me but Christ working through me. Now I feel far from God. I did tell him to fuck off, remember? And I unfriended his son, Jesus. I feel disillusioned with my former evangelical beliefs. Yet people still tell me I'm an inspiration. Kid Cook tells me that he has begun to care about people because of me. A female customer tells me that she reads my blog posts and that they give her hope. My manager at the pub tells me that I've played an important part in her spiritual life and that she's convinced that God brought me to this pub for a reason.

What the fuck? I thought I told God to fuck off?

Sitting in my hot tub tonight, I wondered if perhaps I've borrowed Kid Cook's anger, and he's borrowed my hope. He's always using power words and telling inanimate objects to fuck off.

(after the Canucks beat the Oilers, resulting in him owing me a Fireball whisky shot): "Fuck off, Oilers."

(after we ran out of tartar sauce on fish and chips night): "Fuck off, fish and chips."

(after I dropped a ramequin on the floor): "Fuck off, ramequin."

He's got a lot of anger. I like it. I find a part of me wanting it. I want to be angry. I like being angry. I used to try and change the world. Now I'm just mad at it. And it feels good.

"Freebird" by Lynyrd Skynyrd is one of Kid Cook's favorite songs.

This bird you cannot change.

Lord knows, I can't change.

Lord, help me, I can't change.

I want to be a free bird. But maybe my freedom will begin with me being an angry bird. I like being mad at Christians for their apathy. They don't care anyway. And I'm mad at well-meaning but foolish people for telling me that they're available if I want to talk. People I have no relationship with. I find it condescending. Most of all, I'm mad at God. But apparently, he's not mad at me. Despite my anger toward God, I'm still helping people. How did that happen?

I think it has something to with faith, hope, and love. That's how I've been trying to live my life since childhood. That three-pronged anchor goes so deep that even my anger can't dislodge it. Here's what I mean.

Faith: I'm trusting that something Jesus did in the past gives me and everyone else in the world a secure relationship with God, even if they have anger issues.

Hope: I'm hoping that in the future, everything will be fine for me, my family, and for everyone else in the world, even if they use power words when they talk with God.

Love: I'm believing that everyone I meet in the present is important and worthy of respect and grace, even when they piss me off.

Somehow, if a person has these three things, he or she can't help but end up having a meaningful life. It's some kind of fool-proof system that always makes the world a wee bit better. Faith (past), hope (future), and love (present). I hope my kids figure out how to work that system. It's a life full of hope and free of guilt.

A customer left without paying his $75 bill last night. My manager was worried that she or I would have to pay it. Around 2 a.m., while I was in my hot tub, she texted me. (I still have a few days left before my phone is disconnected.)

My manager texted me: *Did he pay?*

Me: *Nope. He left never to be seen again.*

Manager: *You should have kept his visa card. I'm not paying a $75 bill.*

Me: *I didn't have the energy to battle him. I'm a free bird. The boss can fire my ass. I don't care :-)*

Manager: *Me either. But 75 bucks out of my pocket! Ouch!*

Me: *Don't fucking pay it. Fuck the man. It's illegal to make servers pay for customers who dash.*

Manager: *I will hunt him down!*

Me: *Lol. I'll get the Neighborhood Ninja to help. Why aren't you sleeping?*

Manager: *I can't! Will you call and tell all these demons to fuck off!!! Seriously bri. HELP!!!*

Me: *What's the demon's phone number?*

Manager: *250-666-6666*

Me: *They have a 250 area code? Weird. Hey, Be free, ok? It's easy. Faith, Hope and Love.*

Manager: *K baby. gotta sleep. I love you so much!! Am so thankful for you!!! Honest to God!!!*

Me: *Me too. Remember…free bird.*

I was hanging out with Neighborhood Ninja this afternoon as the sun was sinking behind Maple Mountain. It got cold fast. "Why is it so cold?" I asked. "It was warm a few minutes ago."

"It gets cold fast as the sun goes down behind the hill," Neighborhood Ninja replied.

"Then fuck off, Maple Mountain," I said, as serious as possible.

"You're being hill-larious," he replied.

Will I stop being an angry person? Doubt it.

Will I stop helping people, like a human version of the Littlest Hobo? Doubt it.

Will God fuck off? Doubt it.

And that makes me kind of glad. But in an angry sort of way.

Remember: Free Bird.

CRISPY RICE

Chemotherapy began last week. The nice chemo nurse invited me to sit in a giant blue reclining chair, found a nice big vein on top of my right arm, and inserted the long needle. Then the cytotoxics began flowing into my blood system. Oh right, I forgot to mention that she put a warm blanket on me. I love those warm blankets. I wish someone would get me a blanket-warming oven for home use. And please don't suggest I warm up a blanket in the clothes dryer. It's not the same.

Most people have heard someone say the word "chemotherapy," but few know what it means. Basically, it's the introduction of toxic chemicals into the bloodstream, taken both intravenously and orally. They target and destroy fast-growing cells, such as cancer cells. The main side effect of chemotherapy is that the immune system, also made of fast-growing cells, is damaged for a while. Like choosing to fire on your own troops and the enemy troops at the same time, all the while knowing that your troops will bounce back once treatment is over, leaving the enemy troops damaged and depleted. Like a kid doing a jimmy-flip in a bouncy castle. He's down but not for long.

Chemotherapy is complicated.

Chemotherapy #1: Vincristine is the clear liquid that was injected into my bloodstream for about forty-five minutes last week while I was lounging in the puffy blue chair. I get to have this intravenous injection approximately twice a month over the next six months. Constipation is one of the side effects. 'Nuff said about that.

Chemotherapy #2: I take Lomustine capsules as a single dose on the same day as the first cycle of intravenous chemotherapy. I swallow about six of these giant capsules later that day. I get to do this about five more times over the next six months. Side effects are nausea and a rapid decrease in white blood cells and platelets. To treat the nausea, I take a bunch of anti-nausea pills for the first four days after each cycle. A further side effect is that I get to feel more tired and dizzy, and my legs get to feel wobbly. So, I try to rest a lot. (Lana suggests that increased irritability is also a side effect, but that suggestion just makes me mad.)

Chemotherapy #3: I take Procarbazine capsules each night for about thirteen days after I've finished the Lomustine capsules. The side effects are the same as for Lomustine. The main difference is that, while on Procarbazine, I can't eat or drink anything containing yeast, dairy, fermented fruits, or alcohol. These products contain something called tyramine. which interacts badly with Procarbazine. So, I eat a lot of fresh vegetables, fresh meats, wraps, and Rice Krispie squares. I've developed a craving for Rice Krispie squares in lieu of not being able drink apple wine, snack on nachos with melted cheese, or eat grilled hamburgers on warm yeasty buns. Rice Krispie squares are my new recreational drug.

The reason the oncologists have me doing three different chemotherapies is this: if my cancer cells are resistant to one of the treatments, hopefully they won't be resistant to all three.

To save a bit of money while on my new diet, I've started purchasing no-name Crispy Rice instead of Kellogg's Rice Krispies. The no-name product is at least one dollar cheaper. I poured Hudson a big bowl of the stuff for breakfast.

"Dad, you poured me too much…(pause as he looked at the cereal box)…Crispy Rice," he stated hesitantly.

"Crispy Rice," Ellie said, giggling. "That's funny."

"Sorry, son, for pouring you too much Crispy Rice."

One further side effect of chemotherapy is fevered sleep and insomnia. A few nights ago, I had a fever dream about working at the pub. I was selling teriyaki chicken wings to actor Brad Garrett, but he refused to pay. I knew I was going to get charged for them by my evil bosses if he didn't change his mind. In this dreamscape, my bosses believed the staff were constantly scheming about how to steal from the pub and, therefore, needed to be tightly policed through a series of close-proximity cameras and frequent phone calls.

The problem in my nightmare was that instead of twelve chicken wings, the order came out for fifteen wings. Brad Garrett only wanted to pay for twelve.

"Fuck off, Brad Garrett," I said in my dream. "Just pay for these wings. I'll throw in a beer. By the way, you were great in 'Til Death. Your interactions with Kenny were hilarious."

After a while, I realized I was actually at home and that it was two in the morning. I was not at work attempting to sell fifteen teriyaki chicken wings to Brad Garrett. Since I was emotionally riled up and unable to get back to sleep, I got out of bed, made some Crispy Rice squares, ate a bunch of them, and went into my hot tub. Once back into bed, I fell asleep around 4 a.m. Needless to say, I was fairly tired at 6 a.m. when Lana got up for work.

In the hot tub, I sang this Linkin Park song to myself. It's called "In the End."

> Time is a valuable thing
> Watch it fly by as the pendulum swings
> Watch it count down to the end of the day

The clock ticks life away
I tried so hard
And got so far
But in the end
It doesn't even matter

During my waking hours, I've been continuing my research into the ancient story of Jesus. I've discovered two terms that have proven helpful to me:

Term #1: "The Jesus of History." Even atheist historians agree that a person named Jesus lived in the Middle East two thousand years ago. Jesus probably considered himself divinely chosen by God to dramatically alter history. He was eventually killed for political reasons. He denounced selfish leadership and invited everyone to love and forgive. One scholar, N.T. Wright, argues that the Jesus of History believed that by dying on the cross, he was absorbing God's wrath against the sins of the nation and showing the world a new way to live - a way of love and sacrifice.

Term #2: "The Jesus of Faith." After Jesus' death and subsequent disappearance, groups of believers started worshipping him as the promised suffering Messiah and eventually as divine. As time passed, exaggerated oral stories about Jesus' words and deeds were circulated. Eventually anonymous editors translated these oral traditions into Greek, the language of the Roman Empire. These stories were edited for theological purposes, not for biographical accuracy. These documents include what Christians refer to as the gospels— Matthew, Mark, Luke, and John. In these documents, Jesus is seen as the sinless Son of God, the second member of the Trinity, pre-existent and eternal Creator of the universe, who is coming again in the future to deal triumphantly with sin, suffering, and death. None of these miraculous or supernatural claims can be proven through historical methods. They must be taken on faith.

N.T. Wright puts the terms together in a helpful way: "This historically reconstructed sequence of events (Jesus of History) will not conform fully to the telling of the story that the Gospel writers themselves have offered the Church (Jesus of Faith). The Gospel writers wrote in the context of the evolving Church and sometimes skewed their portraits to match ecclesial interest rather than historical reality."

Jesus would not have believed our current versions of the Christian faith. But it doesn't seem to matter, because it's been over two thousand years, and scholars still can't agree on what Jesus said and did. If accuracy and certainty mattered to God, then God would have left clearer instructions and directions. Clearly, he didn't. Thus, I'm left with at least two possible conclusions:

1. God took care of things through Jesus in ways we don't understand, and God doesn't give a shit if we figure it out or not. He's just happy with the outcome of Jesus' accomplishments.

   or

2. The Christian god isn't real, and the faith based on Jesus is manmade. He wasn't divine, he didn't rise from the dead, and he isn't coming back.

A dear friend sent me a quote by Flannery O'Conner: "The truth does not change according to our ability to stomach it."

Which is harder to stomach: the possibility that Christianity is manmade or the more interesting possibility that Jesus was indeed the promised Jewish Messiah who saved humanity in a manner that has never been fully understood? I find truth in both options.

It's moments like this when I long for a real drink instead of a Crispy Rice square.

THE SPECIAL

I think I know why evangelical Christians are against gay Christians: disgust. Sure, they back up their homophobia with Bible verses, but the select verses just mask their disgust. And because evangelical Christians are generally myopic and egotistical, they believe that gay sex disgusts God too. God is an evangelical, isn't he? That's why he wrote those Bible verses.

I don't think like that anymore. The God I've experienced in this life appears unconcerned with what happens in the bedrooms of consenting adults. In fact, he appears unconcerned with most of our personal decisions.

During the last church leadership meeting I attended before I retired from paid ministry, the few of us who remained on the leadership team, after the exodus of those who didn't think I was a good pastor, were hammering out what church membership consisted of. I was so tired of talking about church membership. Why did it have to be so complicated? Couldn't we just accept into membership everyone who loved God? Nope. It's never that easy in church.

"On top of believing in Jesus, sin, God, forgiveness, and the inerrancy of the Bible," one of the church leaders said, "I think all members should believe that only heterosexual Christians should have sex—and only with their spouses."

"Um," a different leader said, "shouldn't that belief be a goal, not a statement of faith? And shouldn't it be in the section about lifestyle choices, not in the section about doctrine?"

"No," the first leader said. "We need to put our foot down and declare God's views on sexuality."

"Why don't we just require members to listen to God?" I asked. "If he wants them to stop having gay sex, he can tell them himself. Why should we do it for him? What if we're wrong?"

"You're wrong," the first church leader said. "We must draw a line now, so our children know God's truth about homosexuality."

"Our children will never believe your version of God's truth about homosexuality," I replied. "The battle against homosexuality was lost when *Glee* went on television and that Macklemore song went viral. Your kids will never agree with your views when they reach adulthood and become the next leaders at church."

"You're probably right. But at least it won't happen while I'm alive."

"Okay. Fine," I said, like a man knowing when he's lost. "I'm tired. Let's write it up in the way you suggest, sit on it for a week, and come back to discuss it at the next meeting."

"Sounds good, Brian," everyone agreed.

The next day, we all received an email stating that the church leader quoted above had resigned and left the church with his family: *This church has been getting more and more liberal since Brian joined. We can no longer remain as members.*

I resigned five seconds after I read his email. Over fifty people had left the church in the previous six months. That number would only increase the longer I stayed. I was tired. My jaw kept locking painfully because of the stress I was under. I did not sign up for this. I quit.

Why do I share this story? Because last week I had a bare-body massage five blocks from Disneyland. It was the second massage of my life.

The first professional massage I ever experienced was in Victoria three years ago at the urging of my wife. I was very hesitant to have a massage, because I didn't want a stranger rubbing my bare body.

But Lana persisted. So, finally, I relented. On one condition: Lana had to ensure that my masseuse would be female. If someone was going to touch my body other than my wife, I wanted it to be a woman. No woman (or dude) other than Lana had ever touched my body. She was the only woman who'd ever seen me fully naked.

I support gay marriage and gay unions and Gays for Jesus. I'm on board with all that shit. I believe that the bits in the Bible that are used against healthy homosexuality are bullshit.

I'd just be more comfortable with a woman touching my body.

"Come on, Brian," she said, "I'll even pay for it."

"Okay," I agreed, "but if it's a dude, it'll be the last massage I'll ever have."

"Are you homophobic?"

"Maybe. But I don't think so."

"Okay. I promise it'll be a woman," she said. "Do this. It'll feel so good."

"Okay, Lana. I trust you."

It was a dude.

It was an uncomfortable hour. It did not feel relaxing.

Lana apologized later for a promise broken, but I kept my vow. No more massages. Until last week.

We were on our holiday in Anaheim. Lana and I were on a date night, the first in a year, and we had made plans to hit a massage parlor, then dinner and a movie. My mother was babysitting our kids at the hotel. We booked a combo massage. They called it the "Special." Once again Lana promised me a female masseuse.

"Let me double check that it's a woman," she said.

"Okay," I agreed. "Also check that the 'Special' isn't a rub and tug."

"I will."

She came back with a renewed promise that everything was above board and that I'd have a great massage from a nice female masseuse that wouldn't be a rub and tug. I thanked Lana for doing her due diligence. We said goodnight to our kids and to my mother and headed over for our special night.

The toughest decision was what to wear under the towel. Commando or no commando? In Victoria, I hadn't had the courage to go commando.

But this time I figured that since Lana was in the room, I'd be safe to go commando. So, I took my underwear off, put the towel over my bare butt, stuck my face in the massage hole, and waited for the second massage of my life.

The masseuse was indeed a woman. A sixty-year-old Asian woman. With incredibly strong hands.

It was awesome.

And yes, she massaged my bare butt. My cheeks never felt better. Afterwards I felt like running a race. I knew that with my rejuvenated glutes, I could beat anyone.

And no, there wasn't any rub and tug.

Even when the tough elderly Asian masseuse asked me to roll over so she could massage my face and the front of my thighs, she discreetly steered away from my penis. I felt so comfortable with her there was absolutely no erection.

Best. Massage. Ever.

Lana had kept her promise.

The moral of the story? Some promises should be kept, and others should be discarded. Same with beliefs.

And it's also important to point out that Jesus never condemned homosexuality, or bare-butt massages.

THE TOWER OF TERROR

A few weeks ago, we were at Disneyland. One of our funniest memories was when Ellie passed out on the Tower of Terror. The ride does not merely involve falling from truly dizzying heights; it is pulled down as it falls, resulting in everyone on the ride flying into the air and being held in place by seatbelts only.

After our ride was over, Ellie leaned over and told me something: "Daddy, I think I just died and came back to life."

"Yeah," I whispered back, "that's called passing out."

"Okay, Daddy."

"By the way, it's good to have you back."

Sure enough, when we looked at the photo taken at the utmost height of the ride, I saw Hudson and I looking at Ellie from one side, Lana looking at her from the other, and Ellie sound asleep in the middle. We were laughing; she was comatose. She refused to ride that one again. She never complained about it. She just had no interest in dying. Can't blame her.

That's the one rule about Disney: no complaining. Why? Because it's the happiest place on Earth. Many people have never been privileged enough to go. It's like complaining about your diamond ring. Sure, there's lots you could complain about at Disney: the rain, the cold weather, the travel, the line-ups, the big costs for everything, the nickel and diming (Fifteen dollars for a stroller rental? Nine dollars for a hot dog?), the corporateness....

And, of course, one could choose to complain about this particular irony: the more time you spend at Disneyland—watching Disney, buying Disney—the more unimaginative you become. That's right. The golden wizening rod that perfected the imagination sucks it out of you the longer you gaze at it.

But don't you dare complain about it. That would make you a jerk and a snob.

I agree. Who wouldn't? Disneyland is awesome.

Yet, the double irony is this: being alive is better than being at Disneyland. If they had to choose, most people would prefer to be alive anywhere than dead at Disneyland.

No matter how many lifelike environments Disneyland creates (animatronic animals, talking totem poles, funny perfect families, like the one in *Dog with a Blog*), it can't compare to real life. Real air, real friendships, real sports, and real food. Real is super awesome.

Sure, there's lots about real life that is annoying. I've got a real cat, and I complain about him. I've got a real car, and I complain about it. I get real money at a real job, and I complain. But these complaints are common and generally not frowned upon in our culture. Complaining about one's life is one of the most natural things to do.

Weird, isn't it?

Ellie, our adopted daughter, has a biological brother (same mother and father) who lives in foster care in Vancouver. His name is Nathanial. He's about the same age as Hudson. We try and visit him whenever we're in Vancouver. This past Sunday, Ellie and I drove to Vancouver to spend two hours with Nathanial. We took the early ferry and came home on the late ferry.

As we were saying goodbye to Nathanial, I asked him if he'd like to visit us on the island sometime: "Would you like to visit us at our home sometime this spring or summer?"

"That sounds nice," Nathanial replied. "But I may be busy in the summer. I may have a forever family by then."

A forever family is what the one thousand kids on the adoption waitlist in BC long to have: a family of their own. A reliable, loving, and generous family. A parent (or two) who will love them forever.

Nathanial may not remember his friends' names at school, and he may not know his birthdate, but he knows what he wants. He wants a forever family like his younger biological sister has.

Afterwards Ellie said, "I hope Nathanial finds a forever family, like I did."

"So do I, honey. So do I."

I also hope I never complain again. I still have life.

T-BONED

A new fellow came into the pub last night and told me about a customer named T-Bone who would frequent the bar this fellow worked in as a youth. He was nicknamed T-Bone, because he once took all the lads from the bar to a steakhouse for T-bone steaks. T-Bone was famous for three things:

1. He would get liquored each night and still return to the bar the next morning as sober as a thirsty goldfish. The new fellow was proud of the fact that he would give T-Bone all the free drinks he wanted.

2. T-Bone got upset whenever his chair and ashtray were moved. The new fellow would move T-Bone's favorite chair and ashtray frequently, just to fuck with T-Bone.

3. T-Bone loved to smoke unfiltered Export A cigarettes. They tasted better, I suppose.

I heard the details about T-Bone's life three or four times over the course of the next thirty minutes. The story should have taken thirty seconds.

Thirty-second version: There once was an old man who liked to drink like a trout, smoke like an unfiltered chimney, and eat steaks with the lads. Oh, and he didn't like people moving his shit. The end.

I watched Terry Gilliam's newest movie, *Zero Theorem*, the other day while I was sick in bed with s fever. It took a long time for me to recover from the fever, because my immune system was shot to shit. I've always loved Terry Gilliam's films, starting with *Time Bandits,* and then *Brazil* and *12 Monkeys.* This new film tells the story of a man named Qohen Leth who is attempting to discover, through scientific calculations, if life has any meaning. The screenplay is based on the book of Ecclesiastes from the Bible. In that book, the author (named Qoheleth) also attempts to discover if life has any meaning. Qoheleth doesn't use computers or physics formulas in his investigations but rather explores all the physical experiences available to him at the time. Things like alcohol, sex, and unfiltered cigarettes.

Both film and book end on similar notes:

Film: Life began out of nothing and will eventually end with a black hole of nothing.

Book: Meaningless, meaningless, all is meaningless.

How then should we live if it's about nothing? Eat, drink, and be merry, for tomorrow we die. Oh, and don't move other people's shit.

I was talking with Kid Cook about life and T-Bone after the new fellow finally left.

"So, how do you get through your meaningless life?" I asked, only half serious.

"You know what I do," he replied, slightly irritated. "I write a little each day and drink a lot of alcohol."

"Cool. Me too," I said, trying to keep things light. "Though lately I have been adding one more bit to each day."

"What's that?"

"I take a few seconds each day to praise the Lord. Gets my thoughts off myself for a while, know what I mean?"

"No clue what you're talking about, man," he said, now completely disinterested. "Tell me more about T-Bone."

Hours later, at the end of my shift, Kid Cook and I were listening and dancing to "My Songs Know What You Did in the Dark" by Fall Out Boy. I was drunk on the idea of finally going home, and Kid Cook was drunk on six sleeves of Molson Canadian and one shot of Fireball whiskey.

A constellation of tears on your lashes
Burn everything you love, then burn the ashes
In the end everything collides
My childhood spat back out the monster that you see
My songs know what you did in the dark
So, light 'em up, up, up
Light 'em up, up, up
Light 'em up, up, up
I'm on fire!

As we were singing and waving our arms in unison, Kid Cook looked at me, and said, "Look, Brian, I'm praising the Lord!"

"Yes, you are," I said, smiling. "You're lighting 'em up."

I was sitting in my hot tub the other night thinking about life and God. I realized I don't have much evidence to go on, but I still choose to believe these three things:

1. God is real.

2. Jesus believed he was doing God's work.

3. I feel better when I'm praising him. If given half a chance, I will attempt to convince you to believe and do the same as me.

I've got a dear friend who tells me that until I do my final research, I won't know anything for certain. She means we won't get the true answers to our questions about life and God until we die. She's right, and that keeps me humble.

At the same time, based on the limited research I *have* done, I have to continue praising the Lord.

Qoheleth summarizes his findings like this: "Life as we know it, precious and beautiful, ends. The body is put back in the ground, the spirit returns to God…it's all smoke, nothing but smoke…the last and final word is this: fear God and do what he tells you."

I summarize my findings like this: "If life is like a pack of cigarettes, then I've probably only got a few smokes left, and I will break off each and every filter before I smoke them."

So, light 'em up.

THE BIRD, THREE FISH, AND A RUSTY NAIL

I got into a middle-finger battle with an old man driving a large white truck today as I was driving to Sooke to watch the final Hobbit movie, *Battle of the Five Armies*.

Like most battles, it started innocently enough. A white truck pulled in front of me in the passing lane, and I maintained my driving speed. I guess he thought I was tailgating him, because out of nowhere, he slammed on his brakes, causing me to nearly collide with him. I hammered my foot down, burning another millimeter of rubber off my already bald tires, and changed lanes. As I switched lanes, I opened my moon roof and flipped the white truck a nearly three-minute bird. Not content with being a mild irritant, the white truck swapped lanes to get back in front of me and continued driving at an intentionally slower pace. He was also flipping me the bird. Then I switched into the fast lane and passed him while simultaneously opening my passenger window to flip him many continuous birds. We continued this game of cat and mouse and bird for about fifteen minutes until finally the old man in the large white truck exited the highway for the stinky micropolis of Cobble Hill. As he drove away, I continued to flip him as many birds as possible through all my passenger windows and my moon roof. I wished I was the elusive giant sea squid and could flip six uninterrupted birds at the same time, all the while having one tentacle on the steering wheel and one on the gas pedal.

Some might say I shouldn't flip birds to other drivers while sporting a Jesus fish emblem on the back of my car. I mean, doesn't bird-flipping give Jesus a bad name? Shouldn't I simply forgive the white truck and drive on with my life?

I counter that point with this point: I actually have three fish emblems on the back of my car: a Jesus fish, a Darwin fish, and a Sinner fish. In this instance, I believe the Sinner fish superseded the Jesus fish. As a result, in my opinion, Jesus' name remained intact and unblemished. Besides, he's always been able to stick up for himself anyway.

I was listening to the Christian music station the other day, and the evangelical announcer made a statement with which I no longer agree. She stated that since God created relationships, and that God is, in his Trinitarian form, a singular community of relationships, God is the foremost expert on relationships.

I call bullshit.

No offense to God, but let's not compliment him on things that aren't his strengths. He's got loads of great strengths that should be praised: his genius, his creativity, his dry sense of humor. (Have you heard the joke about how God is like a stand-up comedian playing to a crowd that is afraid to laugh? That kills me.)

But relationships? Not in my experience. He's notoriously distant and confusing—and rarely concise. I would even characterize him as being apathetic and emotionally disengaged.

Jesus, in contrast, was great at relationships. Or at least he was great at relationships with certain types of people. Broken people. Outsiders. Disenfranchised. Jesus was a great friend with these types. But with the powerful, the religious, and the popular? Not so much. The first group hugged him; the latter group hammered him.

A sixty-year-old great-grandmother tends bar with me at the pub. You'd swear she wasn't a day over fifty-nine. She doesn't even have any grey hair.

"There are so many types of religious people: Baptist, Catholic, Jehovah's Witnesses," she told me one time. "Until they all agree on the same scriptures, I'm just not interested in religion."

"Those groups actually all share the same scriptures," I said.

"Really?" she said, her face illuminated with genuine surprise.

"Yup. Have you never read the stories of Jesus?"

"No, actually," she said matter-of-factly, "never heard any of them."

"You're nearly a hundred years old and have never read or heard a story about Jesus?" Now I was genuinely surprised.

"Nope. I guess I'm going to hell then, eh?"

"I doubt it," I told her. "Hell is a concept religious people use to threaten and manipulate other people. If you actually read about Jesus, you'd like him. In the scriptures, nonreligious people like you love him, and religious people like those I used to hang out with hate him."

"I find that interesting," she said.

"It's true," I said, looking directly at her for the first time in the conversation. "In fact, the way I understand the Bible, Jesus even found a way for you to be best friends with God without even believing anything religious. As you stand right now, you could not be closer to God."

"You hear that everyone? I'm one of God's special ones!"

"Yes, you are, Great-Grandma. Now could you grab your walker and scoot over to the bar and make me that Rusty Nail I ordered fifteen minutes ago?"

There was a liquor store across the street from our resort in Anaheim that I frequented last month during our holidays. I discovered a lower shelf in the wine fridge that was filled with old bottles of white wine that had the labels torn or somewhat worn off. I took a chance and bought a bottle of 2005 Canvas Chardonnay for $9. I looked it up later and discovered it was actually worth $26, and it tasted awesome. Two nights later, I rolled the dice again and bought a 2004 bottle of Five Rivers Chardonnay for $8. I discovered it was worth $10. Two nights later, I bought a 2007 bottle of Century Estates Pinot Grigio for $10. It was worth $7. My luck had run out, it seemed. On the last night, I bought a 2006 Rex Goliath Chardonnay for $9. Found out it was worth a whopping $3.99. Tasted like vinegar. But that 2005 Canvas Chardonnay—that was awesome. In fact, compared to the Rex Goliath, it grew tastier and tastier in my memories.

There's this song I like that can't be listened to sitting down. It's "The Blue Song" by Mint Royale.

> *Ooh, right through my head.*
> *I ain't got the blues no more I said.*
> *Step some more I said, pick me up.*
> *I'm thinkin' I got my groove-ay-eh.*

Life is about contrast. If we never had the blues, we wouldn't recognize the groove.

If we never drank the vinegar, we wouldn't appreciate the wine.

If God wasn't so distant, Jesus wouldn't have been such a surprising ambassador for him.

And if we didn't get flipped the bird once in a while, maybe we wouldn't realize how good it feels to be told we're special.

EVERYTHING THAT KILLS ME

My seven-year-old daughter, Ellie, has a stubborn streak and a fiery temper. She expresses these two tendencies on an almost daily basis. Often Lana and I merely shrug. Other times, we shrug and mutter, "Irish people."

Ellie's biological father is Irish. That makes Ellie 50 percent Irish. From what we've seen, her biological dad also tends to get mad and dig in his leprechaun heels.

I recall one of my first visits with Ellie's father, when she was a tiny newborn. I took her to visit him and her biological grandmother, who was visiting from Virginia one hot summer day in East Vancouver. At that point, we were merely Ellie's foster parents, attempting to facilitate her return to her biological parents if they somehow went against the tremendous odds stacked against them and won back custody rights. We were also ready and strongly hoping to adopt her if her parents didn't pull off the impossible. During the visit, Ellie was crying and fussing in her biological father's arms. He was telling Ellie how much he loved her and how he would always love her, but she only responded with louder screaming and crying. He handed her to me, and she calmed down immediately. Call me the Irish baby whisperer. Then he stormed off and waited in the car for his mother to join him. I felt bad for him. He had so much love to give but lacked the capacity to be the father Ellie needed. Ellie's biological grandmother apologized for her son's behavior, thanked me for raising her granddaughter, and then left.

Last week, a couple of hours after an outburst of untethered fury and venom directed at Lana, because she wouldn't let Ellie sleep in our bed, I decided to teach Ellie about the Apostle Paul's secret of anger management. I thought it was time for Ellie to learn Paul's explanation for why we do the bad things we do. I drew a picture of Ellie and made a line down the middle of her. On one side of the line, I described all the beautiful things she does (hugs, forgiveness, sharing, and so on), and on the other side, I described some of the negative tendencies she shows (anger, meanness, rudeness). I was attempting to explain that the real Ellie, the truest version of Ellie, is the good version, not the bad version. But about three minutes into my presentation, Ellie interrupted me: "Dad, this is boring."

"I'm just trying to teach you something that will help you," I said.

"But it's boring," she insisted. "I was mean to Mom, because she said I couldn't sleep in her bed."

"But the Bible says that when we're mean, it's not the real us."

"Well," Ellie said, "it's going to be the real me if I'm not allowed to sleep in Mom's bed."

Obviously, I wasn't getting through to her. Or perhaps what I was trying to teach her was bullshit. Or she was just responding like any typical seven-year-old Irish girl. So, I shifted my approach and told her a different truth: "Ellie, here's the thing. If you want to sleep in Mom's bed, don't ask for permission. Just sneak over there after she's gone to sleep. She'll be too tired to tell you to go back to bed."

"Hmm…good idea, Dad! You're the best daddy ever!"

"You're welcome, honey," I said dejectedly.

I was the best daddy ever but the worst children's Bible teacher ever. And I can live with that.

A year ago, a friend who has been a great support to us, and who is also a fantastic photographer, offered to take our family portraits for free. A $650 value. After much reminding, Lana eventually agreed to accept this very generous gift while our friend was in town recently. She took our portraits on a damp day in a damp park just outside of town. Tonight, we received our first pictures from the damp photographical excursion. In one picture, the four of us are happily stomping through a damp field with smiles on our damp faces in damp color-coordinated outfits.

Moments before that image was captured, I threatened the kids that if they didn't smile nicely for the pictures, there wouldn't be any more playdates, video games, or Christmases. Ever. But you see no sign of threats in the picture. You only see happiness.

Such a beautiful family. Such a caring-looking father. It's a gorgeous picture.

It's all horseshit. And yet, at the same time, it's not. The smiles are genuine. We just like to roll through life on impossibly square tires. Life is full of contradictions, and I'm good with that. There is no easy explanation for why we do what we do. We love each other, and yet we fight and hurt each other moments later.

I was in my hot tub last night listening to "Counting Stars" by One Republic.

I feel something so right
By doing the wrong thing
And I feel something so wrong
By doing the right thing
I couldn't lie, couldn't lie, couldn't lie
Everything that kills me makes me feel alive

I was listening to sports radio this afternoon on the way to my final chemotherapy injection for this cycle (four injections down, eight to go) and heard the tail end of an interview with hockey writer Darren Dreger. In the interview, Dreger was complaining about trolls who had been tweeting bile at him for his hockey views and even for misspelling certain words. They told him to fuck off and go to hell for misspelling a word. "What the fuck?" Dreger said. "I'm a bastard who doesn't deserve to live, because I misspelled a word in a tweet?"

He didn't understand why people would do that.

I don't try to be good anymore. I can't change who I am. But I can allow myself to be changed, as I find quiet moments to pause and reflect.

I've been reading Henri Nouwen's book, *Reaching Out*. In it, he argues that loneliness causes us the most trouble in life. Our loneliness drives us either to hostility or to solitude. Hostility leads us to hurt and pain, while a healthy solitude can lead us to a hospitality that brings healing not only to ourselves but also to those whom we welcome into our midst.

In other words, we're mean, because we're lonely.

But the solution isn't to make more friends. The solution is to find ourselves, by ourselves, and to learn to enjoy being in that place of solitude. Only then do we have something to offer our friends. If we have nothing to offer, we will only find ourselves taking from our friends—and being angry when what they have to give isn't enough.

Sometimes I think about myself and my life, and I wish for more. I wish for a better life. I want to be happier. I want to be healthier. It's times like this I realize the truth about myself. I need more solitude in my life.

I don't need to leave my family and start again. I don't need to find a more compatible woman. Or better kids. Or a life with no kids.

My unhappiness stems not from my ethnicity or my parents' influences or even from the Government. It's something deeper. Deeper than a proctologist can discover through a rectal examination. I need to find myself in myself, not in other people or through dramatic life changes. I contain the problem and the solution within me. I need solitude.

And if that sounds boring to you, I can live with that too.

Part Five

ANOTHER DIMENSION

A million miles away

Your signal in the distance

To whom it may concern

I think I lost my way

Getting good at starting over

Every time that I return

Learning to walk again

I believe I've waited long enough

Where do I begin?

Learning to talk again

Can't you see I've waited long enough?

Where do I begin?

—FOO FIGHTERS

COWBOY COLLEGE

This morning, I woke up at 2 a.m. in a pool of sweat. I was having a fever dream that Julian Noir and Howard Moon from *The Mighty Boosh* were stealing my identity, and no matter what I did, they were always one step ahead of me, replacing every part of my life with themselves. It was exactly like that season-three episode, "The Power of the Crimp," except it was me that was being copied.

At one point in my delirium, I turned to Lester Corncrake and asked, "Why me? I'm nobody. I'm not even a good Christian anymore. Why are the Mighty Boosh trying to replace me?"

"Isn't it obvious, Brian?" Lester Corncrake said. "They're trying to copy you, because you're special."

Some of my old Christian friends are concerned about me and my recent theological decisions. One guy messaged me: *I'm surprised at the direction your beliefs have gone. I will continue to pray for you.*

I messaged him back: *Thanks. This new version of myself is merely the eventual and inevitable progression of the person I used to be. It was only a matter of time.*

I don't feel like I chose to be who I am now. It just happened. But it still raises many questions about if I'm a good Christian or not. Sometimes I just want to stop asking questions altogether and run away and escape it all.

I've begun texting again, so I texted Lana yesterday that I want to go on an adventure. I want to travel to Israel. Or move to New York City. Or be that rodeo cowboy from that song, "Like A Cowboy," by Randy Houser.

I feel lost, I texted. *I want to go to cowboy college. I've always wanted to be a cowboy.*

Lana: *You'll always be my cowboy.*

Me: *Thanks, honey.*

Lana: *You should go travel for a year.*

Me: *Thanks. But you know I'm too broke to do that. But thanks all the same.*

Lana: *You're welcome, cowboy.*

Me: *By the way, you'll always be my Shotgun Rider.*

Lana: *I know that already, dear.*

Sometimes I worry that this new version of me is now unemployable for anything other than a low-end bartender job in a small town on the edge of the looniverse. At other times, I feel confident that this new version of me would make the ideal pastor for this world in which we live. I even applied for a church job in a big city the other day. I never heard anything back from them, but it felt good just to have the momentary lapse of self-doubt and confidently put myself out there again.

The other night at the pub, just before I was about to lock the doors after two hours of no business, four good-looking women ran/staggered up the pub patio stairs and hollered: "Are you still open? Please be open. We just came from a sex-toy party and want to do some more drinking!"

"Of course," I said, after an extremely short pause. "We're open!"

A guy can get a lot of attention when he's the only man in the room with four half-cut women from a sex-toy party. They were shouting over each other just to talk to me. And I got some pretty good tips, too.

At one point, one of the ladies, who had fallen earlier that evening and was complaining about a badly bruised behind, asked if I could rub her butt. I politely declined, saying I had some dishes to do.

Not the kind of adventure I've been looking for.

Or the type of employment I'm seeking.

One of my favorite church memories was singing "Don't Worry Child" by Swedish House Mafia with Mrs. Kitchen three years ago at a Sunday morning service.

> Don't you worry, don't you worry, child.
> See heaven's got a plan for you.
> Don't you worry, don't you worry now.

Lana was having some doubts about her upcoming career change a while back. She's becoming a professional family mediator while keeping her job with Canada Post.

I'm so worried about this mediation I'm doing tonight, she texted. *I'm going to fail! I'm not good at this!*

Me: *Just trust in God, dear.*

Lana: *I don't even know what that means!*

Me: *Trust in me then. You rock at mediation. You're going to hit a fucking home run and help a shit ton of people. Own that truth, dear.*

Lana: *Thanks, Brian. You're the best.*

I used to believe that God was always one step ahead of me, planning my career and life choices. I don't believe that anymore.

We're all just wanderers in this looniverse, desperately seeking meaningful ways to contribute. And we're all probably doing a lot better than we realize.

THE LIST

An older woman in a mauve sweater offered up a ten-minute prayer at church yesterday. It reminded me of my childhood, when such long and lonely prayers were the three-services-per-week norm. I turned to my friend and whispered, "That woman is good at praying."

"A little too good, if you ask me."

"No kidding," I said. "I wonder if God likes this marathon prayer."

"It's more like a series of sermonettes than a prayer," my friend whispered back. "And I'm sure God just adores it."

"Do you think she's spitballing this?" I said. "Or do you think it's memorized?"

"It's like the preacher said last week," my friend replied, "don't keep the wine in the bottle for too long, or it'll go bad."

One thing I'll give that dove-haired prayer trooper: she sounded passionate. That's a word that hasn't been true of me lately. A more appropriate word for me would be "list-less" - having a lack of list. "List" being the obsolete term for desire. Basically, having a deficiency of passion for life. I find myself fighting bouts of apathy, anger, and acrimony. I sit on the couch doing nothing. I barely care about the feelings of others. Don't get me wrong, if you ran into me at the pub or on the street, I'd probably still look happy and will genuinely care about you. I may even be singing something by Coldplay (out loud) or Meghan Trainor (under my breath). But the other junk is still there, bubbling like dirty grease below a mirrored smiley surface, and I don't like it.

I've picked up some extra shifts in the liquor store to help pay off some holiday debt and to replace a bunch of shifts I missed last month due to illness. My lack of list has resulted in me not even being upset about working six days a week again. I still get bored by the incessant insanity of bar life, but not as much as before.

Some kids were trespassing in the boss's four-story condo development across the street on the weekend. I looked at the two kid cooks as we watched the young trespassers climb the fence into the boss' castle, and we instantly got excited. We were going to yell at them.

"I see you, motherfuckers!" I shouted.

"You better get out of there right now before we call the police," Kid Cook #1 added.

"We're already calling the cops. It won't take long. It's only three numbers, you dumb fucks," Kid Cook #2 said.

"Fuck the police!" I yelled, getting into it. "We're coming over there to fuck you up ourselves."

"I think they're leaving," Kid Cook #1 said to me, starting to head back in.

But I wasn't done. "You better run, you motherfuckers. I know your faces!"

"Simmer down, Brian. They're just small-town kids having fun."

"Fuck off, small-town fun," I said under my breath. It's not that I was angry at the trespassers – I just didn't care how inappropriate I was towards them.

A drunk former regular I permanently cut off several months ago came back to the bar the other night, and I still wouldn't serve him. Another server felt pity on him and served him one Kokanee, and another customer gave him a peach-flavored cigarette. But he was upset with me for still refusing him service. I told him I wouldn't serve him until he came to the bar sober.

"You're a terrible bartender and a worse Christian," the former regular cursed at me. "You should get a pastor job again."

"I may be a terrible bartender," I said, apathetically, "but at least I have a job."

The former regular was stunned into inebriated silence.

So I went in for the kill. It wasn't pretty. But I just didn't care. "Yeah, that's what I thought. Now get out of my bar, you and your peach cigarette."

The second-hardest thing about taking a few extra shifts at the liquor store is figuring out how to differentiate between cigarette packs. Do you know the difference between regular and king size? How about smooth and rich flavor? And don't get me started on the difference between John Players and Players. Even ice cream and potato chips don't have this many options. Why do people care so much about smoking to create so many options for it?

The hardest thing about working so much is being away from home a lot. I'm not upset about it; I just miss spending time with my kids. And I miss having less-rushed conversations with Lana. I have a new appreciation for those who work low-paying jobs or have to be away from loved ones for long periods of time.

Someone stole a bunch of roofing materials from my job site the other day. I bought an empty lot in downtown Crofton for $70,000 and have hired Neighborhood Ninja to build a small house on it. That's why it's *my* job site. The goal is to sell the 1,260-square-foot level-entry house, two blocks from the ocean, quickly. I need to make some fast cash and then buy another lot and do it again. Yes, you can say it. This bartending, cancer-fighting ex-pastor is also a land developer.

But it sucks when some small-town jerk-off drives off with my materials. While I wasn't too upset, Neighborhood Ninja sure was. I could see him switching into assassin mode.

"That's five hundred dollars' worth of materials!" he exclaimed in frustration.

Now I was the calming influence. "Welcome to Crofton, dude. Now put your Katana back in its sheath."

I was sitting in my hot tub last night drinking some of the blackberry wine reserve I made last summer from the local patches, when it occurred to me that I have the power to turn this listless ship around. I don't like being mean, insensitive, and bored with life. I was listening to "Burn Out Bright" by Switchfoot at the time.

Does it have to start with a broken heart
Broken dreams and bleeding parts?
We were young and the world was clear
But young ambition disappears
I swore it would never come to this
The average, the obvious
I'm still discontented.
If time was never on our side
Then before I die
I want to burn out bright

It occurred to me that the simplest way to stop being listless is to make a list. So, here's my listful list.

Things that make me happy about life:

1. Fried eggs with melted cheese and Louisiana Hot Sauce.

2. Going to church. Not because it's awesome but because, for a few moments each Sunday, I lose myself in the worship of God. And when church is over, I find myself disappointed that I have to wait another seven days before I can go again.

3. Bringing friends to church with me last Sunday. It's nice to have someone to whisper to during the long and winding prayers.

4. Getting paid to count cigarettes and serve beer. I'm told I'm amazing at it.

5. Working with co-workers who are more compassionate then I am.

6. Receiving a nice email from a dear friend telling me that she wishes I could become her church pastor when her current pastor retires. She goes to a post-fundamentalist church that believes many of the things I now believe. I doubt they'll hire me, but it felt great to be believed in.

7. Being able to take my kids to school in the morning and pick them up after school. Sometimes in the morning, Hudson asks me how work was the previous night. That's special to me. Sometimes after school, Ellie is in a really happy mood. That makes me smile. She's a real crackerjack kid.

8. Lana bringing me supper at the liquor store. She works hard at Canada Post, at studying, and at taking care of her family, so her chemo-damaged husband can get the rest he needs.

9. Having a loyal friend like the Neighborhood Ninja, who I can trust to build my speculation house and help me make money to get my family out of mortgage debt before I run out of time, and my life is over.

10. Checkers the cat greeting me when I get home each night with a purr and a bite.

11. Having a hot tub with killer jets.

12. Having over one hundred bottles of apple, white, and blackberry wine in my cellar.

13. Stars. Back in East Vancouver, we had seven, sometimes eight, stars. Here in backwater country, we have millions.

14. Music.

15. Bluetooth headsets so I can listen in my hot tub.

I was having a conversation with Kid Cook about music the other day at the pub. We both like classic rock from the 1990s—Screaming Trees, Soundgarden, Pearl Jam, Nirvana, etc. I mentioned that humans' capacity for creating and appreciating music is often used as an argument for the existence of a soul. Certain animals may communicate with each other in ways that sound musical, but it isn't poetic or purposely melodic, like 1990s rock is.

Kid Cook said he'd need to think about that one.

It's good to have a soul. But it's better to have a soul that is no longer listless. And mine is no longer listless. Because I made a list. I don't want to keep my wine in the bottle anymore.

SEEDS IN YOUR POCKET

Nobody controls me. Nobody.

In my last church employment, there was a time when I felt I was being emotionally water-boarded and being asked to feel and agree with things that felt very wrong. It must have forced me to grow a spine, because now I can barely believe my inner resolve when people try to make me do anything I don't feel is right. Tonight at the pub, some drunk Crofton gangsters tried to force me to say yes when I felt no. I surprised even myself by the grit and sandpaper I dished out at them. Pity the fools.

"Give me a free shot of Fireball, and I'll give you a big tip," the first thug said.

"No," I said sternly. "You're cut off anyways. Your shirt is wet with Jägermeister, and you can't even stand up straight."

"No one tells me I'm cut off. Now just give me my free shot, and I'll pay my tab, and you'll get your big tip."

"This isn't a garage sale," I reminded him. "We don't bargain. It's fixed pricing."

"No, it's not fixed pricing," the second thug said. "I'm strongly suggesting you listen to us. We'll tell you how things work."

"No," I replied, preparing for battle. "You listen to me. It's a simple system. You order a drink. I give you the drink. Then you pay me for the drink."

"No," the first thug insisted, "that's *not* how it works. This is our town."

"Now you're pissing me off," I said. "Focus now, because I'm only explaining this once: I'm not going to be your bitch. And I don't care if you tip me."

"You're making a big mistake. I respect you, Brian. But it's in your best interest to do what we tell you."

I was about to snap; so I spoke slower: "It's in your best interest to fuck off. Now please pay your tab and leave. Is that going to be a problem?"

"There's no problem. But you'll regret this," the thug said.

"You can't threaten me, asshole," I snapped back. "I won't be your fucking bitch."

Punks. They tipped a total of $2.50 on a $100 tab. That was at 12:45 a.m., fifteen minutes before closing. I finally cleaned up their mess by 1:30 a.m. Remember: many bar servers like me only make nine dollars an hour. We pay our mortgages and feed our children with tips. After the thugs left, two cool customers, dads having a night out, yelled at the punks in the parking lot on my behalf. It's nice to have back-up dads when you need them. But if things had really gotten ugly, I doubt I could have relied on two average dads. I'd have needed to call Neighborhood Ninja.

"Hey, Neighborhood Ninja, trouble with the Crofton mafia. Meet me in the pub parking lot. Bring swords."

"Dude, I'm already here in the shadows to your left."

I've been reading a book about the persecution suffered by Mennonite people, my ancestors, from the atheistic communists in the 1920s, 1930s, and 1940s in Russia. The book is *A Wilderness Journey: Glimpses of the Mennonite Brethren Church in Russia* by Heinrich Woelk and Gerhard Woelk: "In 1937/38 almost all men were taken from our village. The rest remained in fear and trembling until 1941. Then the war broke out and the terror increased…congregations destroyed, ministers exiled, hounded away, even killed. Silently our women bore the massively heavy cross…no end was in sight for all of this. As we could see later on, in hindsight, we had arrived only in the middle of the desert."

My suffering at the hands of the Crofton mafia doesn't compare, does it?

A prayer is recorded in the book: "Great God, show me whether you really exist, or whether my faith is in vain. Oh, if only I could overcome these terrible doubts."

I admire their faith. And I equally respect their doubts. If I had lived then, and I can only speculate about this, I like to imagine that I'd still have believed in God. I'd still have believed that he'd saved me from eternal damnation. I'd even have sung his praises, under my breath at least. But I wouldn't have held out hope that things would turn out well for me. There'd be no miracles, no positive thinking or visualizations of a brighter day, and there'd be no friendly Neighborhood Ninja to back me up. Just pain, then death.

And I can't imagine being so pacifistic that I'd go quietly into the night. I'd probably have been more like this guy who ran.

The Woelks: "One man took a large barrel to the river on a sled, supposedly to fetch water. Suddenly the horse began running toward the other shore with the man following, supposedly to stop it. But the horse increased its speed and did not slow down until it had reached the other shore. When the man reached his horse and sled he was already (across the border) in China; the barrel was found to contain his wife and children."

It's a cool story. It'd make a great movie. But in reality, it was a shitty decision. At least it was for those who witnessed it from the other side of the river back in Russia.

The Woelks: "Those who remained behind were considered to be guilty along with those who had left, although they had not known of the planned flight. Almost all the men were thrown into prison or sent into exile. The ministers were again the first to be taken so that the services had to be stopped. Most of the men vanished without a trace. The families were sent farther north in 1941, into the cold regions of Selemdschinsk and Tchegdomyn."

Can you imagine the guilt for the guy who crossed the river?

The irony is that before the Crofton gangsters showed up, I was giving away free drinks. We had a live five-piece band playing from 9 p.m. to midnight, but there was no crowd to listen to them, just their wives and friends. It was like a private concert. So, I asked the boss if we could give them free drinks to ease the pain, and she agreed.

At one point, I was bullshitting with the front man of the band, the Herbicidal Maniacs, swapping hospital stories. He's recovering from a liver transplant, and I'm going into my third chemotherapy cycle next week. He even dedicated a song to me as encouragement in my battle against cancer. Great bunch of people. I was happy to give them free drinks, but it was my decision.

I enjoyed reading James Bond books as a kid. I don't remember which book this was in, but I recall Bond narrating how to endure torture. He said to never let anyone control you. For example, if you're being forced to dig your own grave, it's always important to carry seeds in your pocket. That way, when no one's looking, you can toss a seed into the empty grave. When your captors command you to fill the grave with dirt to break your spirit, the experience doesn't actually break you. Rather, it works to build your inner resolve, because you chose to dig that grave...to plant a seed. Even when captured, nobody controlled 007. Nobody.

When I tell people about my brain tumor, they often feel sad for me. I tell them not to. Everyone has something wrong with them. And if they don't now, they will someday.

I don't know what's wrong with you. Maybe it's your health. Maybe you're being abused. Maybe some inner demon keeps you down.

I want us to remember what the immortal Michelle Pfeiffer said in the classic 1995 movie *Dangerous Minds:* "There are no victims in this classroom."

We are not victims. We don't need to bitch about our lives or be anyone's bitch. Who knows, maybe there's a friendly Neighborhood Ninja hiding in the shadows. And if there isn't, I know there's always seeds in our pockets.

THE TOP AND THE LINE

I was bullshitting yesterday with Kid Cook after a particularly busy day in the cafe. At the Crofton Hotel is a pub, a liquor store, and a small cafe. I tend to avoid taking shifts in the café, because we serve children there. Kids are sticky, and they drop their chicken tenders and fries. But since I've become broke, I'm less choosy. I'll work anywhere at any time—and do almost anything.

It was a busy day, and I did over $600 worth of sales, which is pretty good for me. But I was tired. I had worked over twelve hours the day before and was at the tail end of an eight-hour shift. I was worn out, spent, and in dire need of laughter—of the gut-splitting variety. So, I cleaned up the cafe and went over to the pub to do my cash-out among friendly co-workers instead of alone in the empty cafe. I had been too busy all day to separate my bills and receipts nicely, so I brought my crumpled-up beach-ball-sized wad of tiny papers with me. I guess I looked silly.

"Nice organizational skills, Brian," a co-worker said, "you must be an Aries."

"I don't give a flying ram's ass about astrology," I replied, a bit too forcefully. So, I tried to tone it down. "And yes, this must look a bit messy."

"Brian," Kid Cook interjected, "it's over-the-top messy."

I didn't really want to talk about my cash-out, or which constellation I was born under. I wanted to smile. I wanted to laugh. So, I changed the subject.

"You know what's over the top?" I asked. "The new Furious 7 trailer. Vin Diesel drives a red sports car out a skyscraper window into a neighboring skyscraper. As the car crashes through the window of the second skyscraper and slides through an art show, Diesel jumps out and barely hangs on while the car falls out the window."

"That sounds a little *too* over the top," Kid Cook said.

"No. It was *way* too over the top. That's why it was so awesome."

"Too much over the top for me, man," Kid Cook said, unmoved.

"You want to know how they made it so over the top?" I offered.

"Yeah, I do," he said.

It was at this point in our conversation that I couldn't think of anything funny to say, so I panicked. "Here's how they made it over the top. The movie people found the top, and then they went *over* it."

"So, let me get this straight," Kid Cook said, sarcastically trying to make sense of my explanation, "they found the top, and then they went over it, and came down on the other side?"

"Yeah."

"When you explain it like that, it does sound awesome," Kid Cook submitted.

At that point, Kid Cook said something sexually obscene. I mentioned to him that what he said was over the line.

"So, what I said was over the line?" he asked.

"Yes," I replied, "it was."

"So, there's a line, and when I said those bad words, I was taking my foot, lifting it up, and landing it on the other side of the line?"

"Yeah. It wasn't over the top, but you did go over the line," I said, slyly.

My kids begged Lana and me to sign them up for a soup-making class last week. So, we sucked it up, paid the $20 registration and sent our little babies off to their first cooking class. That's a small price to pay for dreams of not having to cook at home anymore. In Tuesday's class, they made the chicken soup stock, and in Thursday's, the actual soup. My biggest concern, however, was whether Ellie would get along with her instructor. She got into a fracas with the same instructor last year in a card-making class, and ended up kicking the instructor in the shins. After several attempts by Lana to mediate, the instructor agreed to drop her charges against our little girl. As Ellie strutted into the soup class last Tuesday, I gave her strict instructions to be good.

"Ellie, remember to be nice, and don't kick Amber in the shins again."

"I'll be nice, Daddy, and I won't kick her," Ellie told me, "as long as she isn't mean to me."

"Okay," I said, with pleading in my eyes. "*Please* don't go over the line."

I served a guy in the pub a few weeks ago that took over-the-top to a whole new level. He told me and Kid Cook that he was pissed off at the planet Jupiter, that the Andromeda Galaxy was a bitch galaxy, and that he drove to the pub in a spaceship.

"What do you have against the planet Jupiter?" I asked Spaceman.

"It's not fair that Earth only has one moon while Jupiter gets sixty-three."

"That does seem unfair," I said, admiring his logic. "But there's nothing you can do about it."

"Yeah there is," Kid Cook interjected, "we can go kill Jupiter in his spaceship."

"Yeah. Let's fucking kill Jupiter," Spaceman said, excitedly.

We were so far over the top; I could barely see its tip.

At one point, Spaceman asked Kid Cook to tell him a joke. Kid Cook responded with a joke about a witch and her underwear.

"I don't understand your Mayan joke," Spaceman said.

"Mayan joke?" Kid Cook replied. "I'm from Powell River."

I couldn't even see the top anymore. I think we had just entered that bitch Andromeda galaxy. The top was invisible to my Hubble-telescope eyes.

Spaceman wasn't crazy. He was just a lonely old man looking for a place to have a few laughs. I could relate to him. I like to think we helped him achieve his goal, just as Kid Cook helped me achieve mine yesterday.

The world can be a lonely place. There are probably people all around us who haven't laughed in a long time. They're probably nursing bruised shins. Maybe we're the ones who will give them an opportunity to have a moment of fun.

Maybe it's us who need to go over the top, and over the line.

BLACK ROBE

I have a friend in Calgary whom I'll call Black Robe. Like me, he has left the evangelical faith. He came to visit me recently.

"I just wanted you to know that I'm praying for you," Black Robe said, dead pan.

"Nice one," I replied. "I think people who say they're praying for me are really just praying for themselves to feel better."

"That's what I meant actually," Black Robe said. "I feel really bad that you're sick, so I wanted you to know that I'm praying that God will help me get through this difficult time."

One of the fun things we did together was go to church. In the church service, the preacher shared his thoughts on Jesus' comment that he did not come into the world to judge it but to save it. "Jesus didn't come to judge us. But if we refuse his gift of love, God's judgment will get activated against us," the preacher announced.

This gave me and Black Robe lots to talk about after the service ended.

"So," I began, "Jesus doesn't want to judge us, but if he does, it's our fault?"

"God created hell, where you will burn forever, but he also loves you very much," Black Robe surmised.

"Sounds like a comedy routine I heard once," I said.

"It's like God doesn't want us to make him angry," Black Robe continued, "but if he does get angry, he can't be blamed for it. We activated it, not him."

"I wonder why the preacher didn't just preach on the actual verse, about Jesus not coming to judge us but to save us."

"Are you always so cynical at church, Bri? Why do you go?"

"I like the music. And sometimes there's snacks."

Black Robe and I shared many adventures during the years we went to Bible college and lived in East Vancouver. There was the time we went skateboarding down the long windy streets of Three Hills with a bedsheet in-between us as our sail, the times we went to the Bible college lounge to practice talking to girls, and the time we were shafted by a fat hog on the lean streets of East Vancouver. Black Robe and I knew how to have a good time.

Whenever Lana's not around and I'm alone with the kids, I like to acquaint them with the songs of the Foo Fighters. We were listening to "Walk" the other day.

> *I'm dancing on my grave*
> *I'm running through the fire*
> *Forever, whatever*
> *I never wanna die*

Ellie paused after the song was over and looked up at me. "Daddy, I never want to die, either."

I paused before answering. "You'll never die, honey. I promise."

What is it in me that makes that kind of promise? I've lived a good, long life. Sure, I've got regrets. There are things I wish I had done differently, people I wish I had treated differently. We all have those, especially those of us who take the time to soak in our memories.

But in terms of adventures, I've pretty much done it all. Except for one thing. I've never been part of a movement that changed the world, or even a small town. I've tasted of it but never anything that lasted more than a year or two. Maybe my children will someday.

I want to steal Jesus' teachings back from the evangelicals and give them to the sinners who don't go to church and the cynical saints like me, who have left evangelicalism. I just can't help having this dream.

And I'm not really that cynical. The proof is that I always cry during Tyler Perry movies. Lana and I watched *The Single Moms Club* last month in Anaheim. We both loved it and wished we could start a movement of similar groups. Groups of people that exist to help each other get through the tough parts of life and enjoy the sweet parts of life together.

I was in my hot tub the other day, and I prayed: "God, for all the good I've experienced in my life, I credit you and the world you made. And for all the shit I've caused and experienced in my life, I credit myself and my ancestors. And for Christ's sake, please don't activate your judgment...just keep saving us."

M.R.I.

I began using medicinal marijuana six months ago. I've smoked it, vaporized it, and eaten it in cookies, brownies, even in jujubes. I've tried a water-soluble concoction from Amsterdam, unavailable in North America. I've spent $50 on a syringe filled with concentrated weed called Phoenix Tears. Some say that one rice-size morsel of it each day can cure cancer.

Can it? Who knows. One of my oncologists said that often patients will swear that medicinal bud has cured their cancer. But his opinion is that the weed has just treated their chemo side effects of nausea, decreased appetite, and insomnia, resulting in a healthier body better capable of surviving and thriving during treatment. In other words, as cannabis strengthens your body, it allows radiation therapy and chemotherapy to work better.

Over a month ago, I underwent an MRI scan of my brain to see if my ongoing treatment was having any effect on my egg-yolk-sized tumor. I used to discover the results on the same day, and usually they would tell me the same thing. That my tumor is growing two to three millimeters a year, which is nothing to be overly concerned about.

That was when I was getting treated in Vancouver. Now that I'm here on the Island, things are a bit different. I get scanned in Nanaimo and get the results later in the week in Victoria.

I had a visit with my oncologist in Victoria scheduled for a few days after my scan, but it was postponed, because my oncologist changed her visiting hours. I could no longer get a morning appointment. I had to settle for an early afternoon appointment. And the earliest morning appointment wasn't until nearly a month later. Today.

I could have met with my oncologist later in the afternoon on an earlier date, but I didn't want to. Why, you ask? Why not just get someone else to pick up my kids and take a few hours off work to get the results of this very important MRI scan? I don't know. Maybe part of me was skeptical. Even if it's good news, which it probably isn't, the tumor will eventually grow back anyway. So, what's the point of knowing how the tumor is doing now, when my future is already set?

But probably I was just scared. I don't like having a brain tumor. I don't like having cancer. I don't like thinking about death or having the anxiety of not wanting to waste a day of this short life. Or the stress my sickness is putting on my wife and children. Every MRI, every consultation, every injection, every blood test, every cytotoxic pill, and every oncologist visit just reminds me that there is an intruder is in my head. I don't like to be reminded of that.

All that being said, I did visit my oncologist this morning. And the results were wonderful. "Normally, when I tell people good news," she said, "it means their tumor has stopped growing. But in your case, I have great news. Your tumor has actually shrunk!"

I posted the news on my Facebook account (yes, I'm back on Facebook) and received a lot of encouragement. A few of my Christian friends posted that they were praying for me and that my brain tumor report reminded them that God was good. The implication was that God was healing me, because he's a good god. One cheeky "normal" friend of mine must have also felt frustrated by the naivety of such comments.

She posted: *That's great news, Brian! Science is good!*

Why do I believe people who pray for healing and credit medical healing to a miraculous God are naive?

Twenty-one Christian men were recently beheaded by ISIS on a beach in Libya. I'm sure people were praying for them. Is God still good?

A little child recently crept out of his bed in the States, wearing a diaper, a blanket, and his snow boots. He unlocked the front door and froze to death in the snow after he walked a few blocks. Is God still good?

A friend of mine recently discovered that her cancer is back. Again. Is God still good?

The Bible has a pretty coherent and clear view on sickness and health: both good and bad people get sick and die. God doesn't play favorites. Bad shit happens to everyone, and it's never fair. In fact, sometimes the good people get more bad luck than the bad people. The way I read the Bible shows me that Jesus didn't come to heal us of our physical infirmities. He came to save us from our sin.

Another friend posted his thoughts: *Maybe God isn't good or bad. Maybe God is just God. Like him or leave him, he rolls any way he wants.*

So, why did my tumor shrink? Why am I one of the lucky ones? Was it God? Science? Phoenix Tears?

I'm scared to know.

Because if I do find out in the afterlife that it was God who healed me, I'm going to feel pretty stupid for deleting all those comments on my Facebook account about God being good, because he healed me.

Postscript: I want to make it clear to my readers, and especially to my daughter, whose biological parents both struggle with a disease called schizophrenia, that those who smoke pot are twice as likely to become schizophrenic than people who don't use marijuana. Especially people, like Ellie, who are genetically predisposed to developing that awful disease. For people like her, medicinal marijuana is not a medicine but a poison that may lead to a life battling hallucinations and delusions. And as far as I know, there is no cure for schizophrenia.

DUCK MY SICK

I learned a new power-word expression a while back at the pub: "suck my dick." Apparently, I had riled up a rowdy customer at the bar by asking him to be quiet, or he'd be removed. He continued being rude and unruly, so I told him to go. As he was leaving, he pointed his ruddy finger at me and said, "You can suck my dick!"

Salty language!

Kid Cook #2 asked me later if the rowdy drunk had threatened me. If he had, the cook told me, I could call the police and press charges.

"Is it considered a threat to be told to suck a guy's dick?" I wondered aloud. "It sounded more like an invitation than a threat."

"Brian might be right," Kid Cook #1 said. "It takes a lot of trust to invite someone you barely know to suck your dick."

I've since learned that to be told to suck a dick means to be told you are the lesser, of low or inferior value. I figured I owed it to myself to begin using this expression in its correct context. Below are two examples.

The other day I was going over some numbers with Neighborhood Ninja to figure out what our next building project would be. We were about $20,000 short of our proposed budget—which happened to be the exact amount sitting in my RRSP account.

"Well, there's our twenty thousand," I said.

"You want to cash out your RRSP?" Neighborhood Ninja said, incredulous. "Aren't you going to need that?"

"Nah," I said, bemused. "I'll never have time to retire. Besides, RRSPs can suck my dick."

"Dude, that's rich," Neighborhood Ninja concluded.

Last week I came to work and saw that the Crofton mafia were back, sitting in the pub like a bunch of crooked cats at a fish fondue. Immediately, I grew hot under my holier-than-thou collar. This was going to get ugly. I told my co-worker that I would not serve those mobsters.

"Last time they were here, they threatened me, demanded free drinks, and vomited in the bathroom. They may be your friends, but I don't like them," I said fiercely.

"They're nice guys," my co-worker pleaded. "I'm sure it was just the alcohol talking last time."

"I don't care," I insisted. "They can suck my dick."

"Ha-ha. Let me talk to them."

My co-worker had a talk with the godfathers of Crofton, and then they came up and apologized.

"Brian," they said softly, "we're really sorry. We barely remember that night. Please give us a chance to show you that we're actually nice guys."

"Okay, that's a really good apology," I said, smiling. "I trust your sincerity. I'd rather trust you than hold a grudge anyways."

Later, my co-worker asked me how our conversation went.

"I told them that I wouldn't accept their apology and that as soon as I get a chance, I'm going to fuck them up," I joked.

"I'm sure you did. Thanks, Brian."

As the repentant gangsters left, they invited me to play floor hockey with them sometime. "That sounds fun," I said. "I'm looking forward to laying you flat on your ass."

A friend recently encouraged me to stay true to my core values, as they have gotten me this far in life. I mentioned this to Kid Cook.

"Yeah," Kid Cook said, mockingly. "Your core values sure have taken you somewhere special. You're a shitty bartender in a shitty bar in a shitty town on the edge of shit. Thank you, core values."

So, I asked my friend to clarify what he meant.

"When people hear your name and smile, that means you've had an impact," he said.

"Well, if smiles are the litmus test for spiritual success, I am indeed a successful man," I replied.

Some people think I'm losing my faith, because I have cancer. That's horseshit. I haven't lost any faith. I've lost certainty. I have more faith than I've ever had in my life. You need a lot of faith to believe in God and Jesus and not in the Bible.

And I would never blame God for my cancer. Millions of people have cancer. God doesn't owe me an apology. He's God, and he can lay me flat on my ass whenever he wants. I'll keep praising him regardless.

You see, I am the lesser. And I'm good with that.

And if this chapter made you smile, you can thank my core values.

THIS OLD SHED

Do you like watching bad movies? I do. Tonight, I watched 1997's *Home Alone 3* with my kids while Lana was in Victoria studying. The reason I bring up this cinematic wonder is because many of the main characters used large cell phones and old-tech pagers. I had to explain to my kids what a pager was.

"What is a *paa*-ger?" Hudson asked.

"It's pronounced *pay*-ger, not *paa*-ger," I explained.

"So, what is it?"

"It's also called a beeper. You call a person's pager number, then type in the number you want the person to call you back on. That number comes up on their pager, and then they call it when they get a chance."

"Like the opposite of a smart phone?" Hudson suggested, smirking.

"Smartass."

I had a conversation with my Vancouver radiologist a year or so ago. He told me that the incident rate of people having brain tumors like mine has risen dramatically over the past twenty-five years. I asked him if he thought it had anything to do with those old cell phones many of us used in the nineties.

"That could very well be true," he said, matter-of-factly.

"Those phones sure got hot," I replied sadly.

"Too hot, I'm afraid," the radiologist said, knowing far more than he was admitting.

So, that's what I was thinking about while I watched this movie and saw all those red-hot cell phones. I wondered what life would have been like for me if I wasn't such an early adopter. What if I hadn't used cell phones so much in the 1990s?

Lana and I were talking about death and dying the other day. She's afraid of dying. I'm not. Death has been a part of my life for so long now that I don't worry about it. Part of me actually looks forward to it, because I'm fascinated with what happens next.

"Why aren't you afraid of dying?" she asked.

"I don't know; I'm just not," I said. "I've done everything I've ever wanted to do, I guess."

"What about seeing your children grow up? Get married? Grandkids?"

"Of course, I'd like to see those things. But I know my kids. They're strong, confident individuals. They'll be okay without me."

"But I won't," Lana said, almost in a whisper.

I do have a list of lessons I hope my kids have learned from me:

1. Own your mistakes. Blaming is the weak person's way out. The strong person knows how to say sorry.

2. You are never the most important person in the room. But you do have the most power. Use that power to help the weaker ones in the room.

3. When you get into trouble, you always have two choices: cry about it, or work harder.

4. Everything has a home, and the floor is not a home.

5. Everything you say must be true, but don't say every-thing that is true.

6. Always give your best effort.

7. Never settle for just giving your best effort.

8. Respect everyone. Respect means caring about the other person's feelings.

9. Don't be easily offended, and don't easily offend others.

10. Respect your mother above all.

I was sitting in my hot tub the other night thinking about the stars. The light from the stars is so old. Some of it is over 250 years old. But I'm tired of that old starlight. I want new light.

People live for all kinds of things. Some love adopting new technology. Some love gossiping about other people's lives or bitching about their own. Some love making money, having sexual experiences, enjoying the highs that come from drugs.

But it all seems so old. I crave something new. Not a sequel or a reboot or a warmed-up re-imagining but a Bright Morning Star.

I really like that One Republic song, "I Lived."

I hope that you spend your days, but they all add up.
And when that sun goes down, I hope you raise your cup.
Oh, I wish that I could witness all your joy and all your pain.
But until my moment comes, I'll say...
I did it all
I owned every second that this world could give.
I saw so many places, the things that I did.
With every broken bone, I swear I lived.

There's an old shed on the lot where Neighborhood Ninja is building my spec house. He wanted to tear it down. I wanted to keep it. I won that battle, and it got to stay. But the other day, as I often do, I drove past the house with my kids on the way to their school. As we drove slowly past the house, we saw Neighborhood Ninja standing alone in the old shed.

"What's he doing in the shed?" I asked myself out loud.

"It looks like he's peeing," Hudson said.

"Yeah!" Ellie concurred. "He's peeing in Daddy's shed! Ha-ha!"

"You're right. Neighborhood Ninja is taking a piss in my shed!"

I guess I'd lost after all. I was a fool to think I could battle a ninja and win.

Do you know why living with death is better than living forever? People who live forever take each day for granted. They don't treat each one as special. Those who see life as having an end cherish each day, always looking for new things. We keep dreaming and finding meaningful things to do every day.

It might be time for me to tear down the old shed and build a new one.

And it also might be time to dream new dreams. I've got a lot of life in me yet.

Part Six

INTERGALACTIC

All the buildings, they lean and they smile down on us

And they shout from their rooftops words we can't trust

Like "you're dead, you are tired, you're ruined, you're dust

Oh, you won't amount to nothing, like tanks full of rust"

But we scream back at them from below on the street

All in unison we sing, our time's been redeemed

We are all of the beauty that has not been seen

We are full of the color that's never been dreamed

Where nothing we need ever dies

—LONE BELLOW

DRINKING BLOOD WITH SPACE ROBOTS

I've been struggling over the past three weeks with fever dreams. With my white-blood cell count so low because of chemotherapy, it takes me a long time to fully recover from fevers and the flu. So, for a few nights last week, I'd wake up from sweaty dreamscapes talking with and yelling at, myself.

"Hurry up and serve these hamburgers to the customers lined up outside my bedroom window!"

"It's not real! Open your eyes! Do you see a kitchen in here?"

"Hurry up and serve these beers to the Transformers lined up outside my bedroom window!"

"It's not real! Open your eyes! Do you see any beer taps in here?"

"But Optimus Prime and Megatron are demanding refills of their High Trail Honey Ale!"

"Idiot. Don't you realize space robots don't even drink honey ale?"

I was in church a few weeks ago with my kids and their friend, Squid. Prior to church, we swung by the hospital to have my blood tested, as is my custom. Since Squid wanted to see the blood technician do her job, she and Hudson got to watch, while Ellie hid behind a magazine. A needle was inserted into my forearm, and a pint of blood was removed. Squid was obviously agitated.

"Did that hurt?" Squid asked.

"Not really."

"It's like having a flu shot, but longer," Hudson said helpfully.

"What do they do with the blood?" Squid asked.

"We analyze it to see how many white blood cells he has," the technician replied.

"That's what she says," I joked. "I'm convinced she goes into the back room to drink it with her co-workers."

"We like to make Vodka Caesars with patients' blood," the technician said, smiling.

"And Bloody Marys," I said, taking the joke further.

"That's gross," the technician said, thinking she was ending the sick fantasy. "All done. Where to next?"

"Church," I said, unwilling to let it go. "We're going to sing songs about blood. Thanks again."

"Going to church to sing songs about blood," the technician muttered as she walked away. "That's a good one."

Evangelical people love to sing songs about Jesus' blood. They sing about how it was poured out on them when Jesus died and that it now covers everyone, making them white as snow. Critics of Christian theology often say this type of thinking is rooted in pagan blood religions and can't be characteristic of a loving twenty-first-century deity.

Perhaps. It does sound a bit cultic. At the same time, blood religions slowly became extinct after the time that Jesus lived. None of the major religions today slaughter animals or sacrifice their children to pagan gods. Coincidence? Maybe not.

Perhaps what Jesus accomplished on that cross enlightened humanity, so we left savage religion for good.

I finally had the energy to refill my hot tub yesterday. I had emptied it three weeks ago, because the water stank. As I was lounging in the fresh, clean water after work, I was listening to two cover versions of the classic Ten Years Ago song, "I'd Love to Change the World." I prefer the Philip Sayce version to the Jetta version.

I'd love to change the world
But I don't know what to do
So, I'll leave it up to you

Apparently, at the time the band was feeling powerless to make their crummy 1971 world better. So, they decided to just leave it up to their listeners to find a way to fix things.

I feel powerless to make my crummy 2015 world better.

I live in a small town of two thousand people. Visitors to Crofton often mention how beautiful it is here and that it must be a great place to raise kids. All true. But I've seen the underbelly. This town has family abuse, poverty, racism, environmental destruction, personal brokenness, and spiritual emptiness. Mine included. I don't know what to do about it either.

Who do I leave it up to?

The Bible has been heavily edited by well-meaning people. Much of it is ancient opinion, not divine direction. But I'm convinced there is a golden thread throughout much of it. A thread about love. About the importance of the spirit. About mindfulness. And about oneness.

I have a habit of taking food from the kitchen cabinets and putting it on the counter. Lana has a habit of taking food off the counter and piling it up inside the cabinets.

"Why do you hide food in the cabinets?" I always ask Lana.

"Because it makes a mess on the counter," she always responds.

"True," I admit. "But this is also true: food unseen is food uneaten."

And she ends the debate by saying, "And food uneaten is food gone bad. Thank you, Sensei."

The other day, Lana had a crazy dream. In her nightmare, Neighborhood Ninja was setting me up with a cute ninja girl from his martial arts class. Lana woke up furious at Neighborhood Ninja, but she calmed down after a bit. "Promise me that if Neighborhood Ninja tries to set you up with a new girlfriend, you'll say no, okay?"

"Sure," I replied. "And promise me that if Optimus Prime and Megatron come by your bedroom window in the middle of the night for a pint of High Trail Honey Ale, you'll say no, too, okay?"

What's real? What's made-up? What's truth? And how should I live in a world like this?

I don't know.

But for today at least, I will choose to love as Jesus loved, because we all have been covered by the love of God. And love unshared is love gone bad.

HAPPY FALSE BIRTHDAY

A couple of months back, my supervisor at the pub had a birthday. Her daughter and some of my co-workers surprised her by decorating the pub with banners and ribbons. The banners read, "Happy Birthday, Cyndie!"

It was all very sweet. But it triggered an irrational fear in me. What if, on the off-chance someone discovered my birthday and made the effort, this awful tragedy happened to me? So, I took matters into my own hands and made a preemptive strike. I went onto Facebook and changed my birthdate. Then I promptly forgot about it. Until March 3—the false date I had entered.

Throughout March 3, and belatedly into March 4, I received message after message from friends, family, and acquaintances, all wishing me a happy birthday.

Well-Wisher #1: *Happy B-Day! Keep looking up!*

Well-Wisher #2: *Happy Birthday, Brian! You are an awesome light!*

Well-Wisher #3: *Wishing you all the best on your birthday! You deserve it!*

And, of course...

Well-Wisher #4: *May God bless you on your special day!*

At least 140 people praised me and wished me well on my false birthday.

I felt like an asshole for deceiving my seven hundred closest friends. But it was too late to do anything about it. So, I stayed the course. And when the day was over, I did the most sensible thing I could think of: I changed my date of my birth on Facebook again, this time to April 3.

I was born on May 3.

I know. I'm a bad person. But I had to see what would happen if I repeated the social experiment.

You guessed it. On April 3, I received another one hundred birthday wishes.

The best and worst part was that many of them were from the same people.

Well-Wisher #1: *Happy birthday, Brian! May the years to come be as wonderful as today.*

Well-Wisher #2: *Happy birthday, Brian. Didn't you just have a birthday a couple of months ago? How time flies!*

Well-Wisher #3: *Happy Birthday again…! Lol Don't know how I mixed that up*

And, of course, this one:

Well-Wisher #4: *Happy Birthday, Brian! I hope your day is filled with laughter.*

It was.

I used to dislike getting older. Each birthday reminded me of the limited number of years I had left. But now I don't give a shit. I just imagine that I'm a happy ninety-year-old and will soon be dying after having lived a good long life. That's why I call the old men at the pub "brothers" and the old ladies "girls." I feel an affinity toward them. I view them as my peers. We have something in common: we have far more years behind us than ahead of us.

Lana tells me that I shouldn't write about death so much. But I figure, why the hell not? No one else I know is.

One of the interesting things about writing about my demise as much as I do is that I'm starting to get a steady stream of visitors coming over to the island to visit me and pay their last respects. Old friends from years gone by. It's awesome, actually. I'd probably not be able to visit them if I was perfectly normal and healthy. We'd all be too busy with life. But I'm not healthy, and so they come. We share stories. We bullshit. And it's very affirming. You should be so lucky.

Someone once asked James Gunn, the director of *Guardians of the Galaxy,* how he made such great movies. In the interview, he described an awakening he experienced after helping write the script for *Scooby Doo.* During his epiphany, he realized he should make art not to be successful but to make others happy. "I'm not only on this planet for myself, but for other people," Gunn said in an interview, "and that by serving others the best I could, that's how I could be the happiest."

And that's when he started writing the most entertaining movies of his life.

As I enter my final ten years or so, I'm left with a couple of options: I could slink away into oblivion, focusing solely on my family, or keep trying to serve others and tell them about Jesus. It'd be easy to do the former, but I'm driven to keep doing the latter. Why?

Reason #1: Because Jesus was still a rad person who may have been divine and just may have saved the people of the world from personal and cosmological destruction.

Reason #2: Because people are still sad, short-sighted, and unhealthy. If they knew how fantastic Jesus was, they would follow his teachings. They would even discover the joy that comes from praising Him. Praising God distracts us from the awful business of judging others and losing ourselves.

I enjoyed hearing this Bible verse in church this morning. It's from John: "Jesus is the atoning sacrifice for our sins, and not only for ours but also for the sins of the whole world."

If God has forgiven everyone without us even realizing it, I have a responsibility to tell people about it.

Norman Cousins was a famous journalist, author, and activist who suffered from several life-threatening illnesses. He was a firm believer in the power of positive thinking, especially the healing power of laughter. His doctors claimed that many years were added to Cousins' life because of his commitment to faith, hope, love, and laughter. One interesting thing about Cousins is that he would frequently watch Marx Brothers' movies before going to sleep, claiming that ten minutes of laughter was better than any painkiller.

He also had an opinion on forgiveness. Cousins wrote: "Life is an adventure in forgiveness."

I like that a lot.

And in case you're wondering, I don't feel bad about deceiving so many people with my false birthdays. Facebook is mostly bullshit anyway. And it was pretty funny, at least to me. I hadn't laughed that hard in a long time.

I think it may have even added a year or two to my life.

THE LIVING YEARS

I had a dream visit from my dead father last night. In my dream, I was returning home from my job as an extra on the set of the television show *Doctor Who*. Some of the crew were with me. When I got to my parents' house, my father was there, just as I remembered him from his final weeks of life.

During those final weeks, he was gaunt and breathed very quietly, half-asleep most of the time. He still had his moments of clarity though. In my dream last night, he was having one of those moments. I entered the room, where he was sitting on the couch, sat down beside him, and put my arms around him.

"I really miss you, Dad," I said tearfully.

"I miss you, too, Brian. I love you very much."

When I was hired as the senior pastor at the church here in town, I was pretty excited. The church members had voted 100 percent in favor of hiring me. It's typical in church votes to reach 85 percent or even 95 percent. But 100 percent? That's rare. After the hiring, one very spiritual woman in the church, who also had cancer, told the church leaders publicly that God had definitely led me to the church and that we had all been blessed overly and abundantly.

But when I told my father about it, his response was less enthusiastic.

"They hired you as their senior pastor?" he said. "I'm surprised. Did they even read your resume?"

"Thanks for the show of support, Dad. Hear that sound? It's the wind coming out of my sails."

"Oh. Um…I'm sure you'll do fine."

I resigned two and a half years later. Too much opposition from conservative groups in the church. I was feeling like the out-of-breath kid in gym class who was the recurring victim of vicious dog piles. I was being accused of being a bad pastor, because I kept pissing off the wrong people. Sometimes patrons at the pub ask me about it.

"You're a bartender who used to be a pastor? How the hell did that happen?" they ask.

"I don't play well with others," I typically respond.

Only two types of people are involved in dog piles: those who jump on the weak kid and those who watch. I'd like to say I came out swinging, but I didn't. I came out cracked and dirty with a punctured lung. On my last Sunday there, the last remaining church leader passed around a bucket to collect a financial love offering for my family and me. It came back empty.

I had an encounter with a local mom about a month prior to my resignation. She had never attended our church and had no clue of the stupid shit that was exploding inside the church walls.

"So, you're the new pastor in town?" she asked. "I can't believe it! You're so cool!"

"Yeah," I responded, looking down. "I've actually been here two and a half years. Not exactly new."

"I had no idea! You must be an incredible pastor, because I heard it's awesome at that church now."

"Are you busy this Sunday?" I asked, looking up. "The church could use some more people like you."

I've always gotten along better with normal people than church people.

I had a conversation with my father a few months before he died.

"I know I wasn't the most affectionate father," he admitted, "but I did try my best."

"Haven't you seen those movies where the dying father starts to cry at the end of the film and embraces his children, telling them how proud he is of them?" I asked.

"That's just in the movies, Brian. This is real life."

I've always liked that Mike and the Mechanics song, "The Living Years."

> I wasn't there that morning
> When my Father passed away
> I didn't get to tell him
> All the things I had to say
> I think I caught his spirit
> Later that same year
> I just wish I could have told him in the living years

One of my biggest regrets in life is not being there when my father died. I arrived ten minutes late. Why? Because I was busy doing church stuff. I was in my office attempting to mediate between a fossilized father and his wayward son, both of whom would be jumping on the dog pile the next year.

I wish I could turn back time. I would have been there in the room when my father passed away. I would have been there to support my mother as she struggled to take care of her dying husband through his final night.

But I wasn't.

Thoughts like these don't depress me or leave me riddled with guilt. Like my father taught me, most of us normal people don't get movie endings. This is real life.

In real life, we're late for our father's passing. In real life, we pounce on each other in Jesus' name. In real life, we don't listen to our children's hopes and dreams.

I've read a lot about not having regrets but instead seeing mistakes as lessons learned. Maybe that's true. But maybe that's bullshit. Because I do have regrets. And I can live with them.

Arthur Miller died of cancer at age eighty-nine. He had a thought on regrets: "Maybe all one can do is hope to end up with the right regrets."

Do you consider yourself a normal person? Then you probably have some regrets. I hope they're the right kind of regrets.

And if you don't go to church, maybe you should consider it. The church could use more people exactly like you.

THE CANDY AND THE GRISTLE

I took my kids back to church this past Sunday. Man, it is *not* getting any easier to be a part of the solution. Church services are so boring.

One of the worst things about boring church services is all the public praying. Jesus made it clear that he didn't support public prayers. He told his followers to pray in their closets. So, why do we do it so much? Stand up, sit down. Up, down, up, down. Boring prayer after boring prayer.

Typical Boring Prayer: "Thank you for the freedom to worship you...please be near this sick person...fill this place with your presence..."

I feel like I've heard the same prayers week in and week out for the past forty-five years. Church services need to be more entertaining. This past Sunday, the preacher said that God had laid it on his heart to preach on the topics of heaven and hell. Why, you ask? Because it's not being preached on enough, he told us. I felt like I was going through purgatory to hell itself. Each evangelical preacher thinks that when they preach on hell, they're being original. They're not. They're being redundant and irrelevant. Like the drunks at the pub telling me over and over again how to bring in more business.

Drunk #1: "Better drink specials."

Drunk #2: "Keno."

Drunk #3: "Live music."

Drunk #4: "Strippers."

Drunk #5: "Cuter bartenders."

I take offence at that last one.

Each time I hear these alcohol-fueled sermons at the bar, I roll my inner eyes, smile, and nod. We all know there are no good suggestions for turning business around at a slow pub in a town of two thousand people.

Preaching on heaven and hell is not going to prevent anyone from going to hell, let alone fill the pews with more people wanting to hear about heaven. Preaching on hell will merely make modern eyes like mine glaze over as I stumble out of the building looking for a different church. One that isn't like a trip to the museum.

All my life, I've heard that church services shouldn't be a show. Why the hell not? God would probably get more glory at an entertaining service than at a boring-as-shit service. I'm talking about playing secular songs about God and the spiritual life, having entrance music for the preachers, utilizing stand-up comedy, and serving more snacks. No more sermons on boring topics like heaven and hell. Until you die, visit those places, and come back with video footage and autographed photos, keep your opinions to yourself. I don't want to listen to your stale theology anymore.

Churches must change or die. They must become relevant and helpful for those of us who are disillusioned, skeptical, and bored with life. There are no tweaks or tune-ups that will turn the fortunes of church around.

I was serving two old ladies at the pub the other day. As I approached their table, they accused me of eavesdropping on their conversation.

"I wasn't eavesdropping," I said.

"Yes, you were, young man."

"Were you talking about leaving your husbands?" I asked.

"No. We did that already."

"Running away and joining the circus?"

"No. Clown phobias."

"Are you about to pull knives out of your pantyhose and rob me?"

"No!" the old ladies shouted. "We were talking about marijuana candy!"

"Oh. The lollys? Or the jujubes? Or perhaps the pink cannabis popcorn?" I queried.

"No. The scotch THC mints. Want one?" the old ladies asked.

Evangelical Christianity is built on a belief that the entire Bible is the authoritative Word of God. Every word, every event, and every idea in the Bible is God's truth. Evangelicals base this bit of theology on a verse written by Paul to Timothy: "Every scripture is inspired by God and is useful."

Most don't know that it can easily be translated a different way: "Every scripture inspired of God is useful."

Notice the difference? Not necessarily all of scripture needs to be considered inspired. That means a bunch of it can be considered as the opinions of people—and that's okay. Because some of it *is* inspired and useful. Eat the meat, spit out the gristle.

How do you tell the difference between the God bits and the human bits? Listen to your heart as you read. Eavesdrop on the spirit of God that surrounds you and flows through you. The inspired stuff in the Bible will come alive. The dead bits won't.

People in our world are still interested in God and Jesus. Many are so tired of the overly sweet spiritual options coming out of our self-centered media-saturated culture that they're even open to learning from—and being challenged by—a partially inspired Bible. We have an incredible opportunity to create a gathering of people who not only learn from Jesus but also have fun together. And change the world together.

When I was twenty years old, I began asking a question and have never stopped asking it. If evangelical Christianity is true, why do so few people believe it, and why are the ones who do believe it so lame? I have believed many different answers to that question over the decades. My latest answer?

Evangelical Christianity is *not* true. That's why so few people believe it. The ones who do believe it are lame, because they've probably believed it since childhood and are afraid to question it. That also explains why they keep their faith to themselves and don't try to convince their friends and neighbors to become evangelicals. It's because they don't believe it deep down in their hearts. And that's lame.

There is another category of people who say they are evangelical Christians. These people find hope and community in the evangelical church. They may recognize the stupid stuff in the movement, but they are so hungry for spiritual truth they knowingly eat the meat *and* the gristle. I respect this category of people, even though I hope they recognize the gristle for what it is and spit it out, as I've done.

And no, I don't want any of your THC candy. I'm hungry for meat.

SPINELESS VERTEBRATES

I completed my fourth chemotherapy cycle a couple of days ago and was feeling tired, so I sat down to listen to a two-hour podcast about the brain, space, and a fellow named Science Mike McHargue. Science Mike had abandoned evangelical Christianity to become an atheist but later traded in his atheism for a more mystical Christian faith. The link for this podcast was sent to me by a friend, who is also struggling with his faith.

In one portion of the podcast, host Pete Holmes talked with his guest, Science Mike, about the brain.

"Every vertebrate has a thalamus," Science Mike explained. "The thalamus is the part of the brain that governs your sense of identity."

"Vertebrate?" Pete asked, not quite understanding.

"That means an animal that has a spine," Mike explained further.

"I feel stupid now," Pete said, irritated. "So, like, not a jellyfish?"

"Right," Mike said. "By scanning brains, we've learned that people who meditate on a loving God have a differently-shaped thalamus than other people. They are less likely to become angry or fearful and more likely to respond with compassion."

"So, even if the belief in a loving God is a sweet myth, by believing it, one becomes a better and more compassionate invertebrate?" Pete responded, starting to get a handle on the idea.

"Vertebrate," Mike corrected.

"Fuck you and your vertebrate," Pete said, even more irritated.

"Maybe you should meditate on God more," Mike responded softly.

By merely thinking about God's love, I will become more loving? That sounds an awful lot like the sanctification process. Like an almost effortless system of behavior modification. I like it.

In the previous chapter, I invented a portion of a conversation that I had with two older ladies at the pub. I asked the ladies if they had ever tasted pink marijuana popcorn. As I wrote that bit, I was trying to imagine the least likely food that could be turned into an edible marijuana product. I thought I was being hilarious.

This past weekend I went to a new medicinal marijuana dispensary in Nanaimo to get some concentrated CBD pills. CBD is a medicinal cannabinoid that contains no THC or other psychotropics—just the concentrated healing part of the marijuana plant. CBD pills have no noticeable effect on me; they merely do their unnoticeable job of shrinking my brain tumor. I have little desire to get high or stoned. I merely want to get better. As I entered the small dispensary, I noticed an odd thing on the receptionist's desk. You guessed it. It was a bowl of…pink cannabis popcorn.

It was a black swan event.

I should have imagined marijuana pork riblets instead of pink popcorn. Or THC-laced roast-beef gravy.

This morning as my kids ate breakfast, I asked them if they wanted to learn something about the brain. They said they did.

"Your brain is like soft plastic," I said. "Everything you think about influences it. For example, if you think about a loving God, you will become a nicer person. If you think about an angry God, your brain will become unhealthy, and you will blow up buildings. Isn't that interesting?"

"Not really," Hudson said.

Ellie took her time before responding. "Checkers should think about God more. Then he won't bite me all the time."

"Good talk, kids," I said dejectedly.

In the podcast interview, Science Mike said that science is better for proving things, and faith is better for giving meaning.

I like that. Science can't prove or disprove God's existence. Of course, if people really probe a belief in God, they will find a shit ton of contradictions and moral objections. But in my opinion, deciding to believe in God and in the saving life and death of his Son is still a better and more beautiful story to believe in than nothingness. I realize that nothingness isn't the only alternative. There are probably over 100 flavors of beliefs available. I still find the sacrifice of Jesus the most beautiful of them all. But that's just me.

And based on those experiences of mine, I'd be a spineless vertebrate not to decide to believe in him.

I've begun praying again. I still go to church, too, but I leave after the singing is over. Sermons make me angry. Praising a loving God makes me happy. And apparently, it makes me more compassionate, too.

I was listening to the Lone Bellow's song, "Bleeding Out," last night in my hot tub.

Breathing in, breathing out, it's all in my mouth.
Gives me hope that I'll be something worth bleeding out.

Then I breathed a prayer: "Lord, here I soak, broken and broke; my life poured out for you. Use it if you want. You've already taken so much, but you can have the rest. You've given me less than I wanted, but more than I need. Thank you."

There are a lot of surprising things in our world. Things like the thalamus, black swans, and pink cannabis popcorn. And finding faith in the jetted hot tub of doubt.

BARTENDER...NO MORE!

The godfather of Crofton came into the pub with his friends the other night. I asked him how his adopted kitten was doing. A lost kitten was running around the pub patio a couple of months ago, when it was really cold. The godfather took her home.

"She's doing really well," Godfather answered.

"What did you name her?" I asked.

"We named her Jo-Jo."

"Nice name," I said. "Thanks for taking good care of her."

"No problem," Godfather said serenely. "She's a great kitty."

The godfather of Crofton is becoming less and less intimidating. Jo-Jo must be softening him up.

A customer with a foul mouth and a rowdy disposition came in that same night. This guy tasks me. He accuses me of under-pouring his drinks and overcharging him at the till.

"I only have forty dollars," the Rowdy said, bluntly.

"You owe me forty-five," I replied, equally as blunt.

"I might have some change. Here's a dollar fifty."

"I'll cover the three fifty," I said, hoping that if I was nice, he'd leave quicker.

"You can cover the entire five dollars then," the Rowdy demanded.

"I notice you've got lots of change. Just give me what you've got, and I'll cover your shortfall."

"You can't have my fucking change. You're trying to steal from me."

"Just pay your bill, please," I said, sternly.

"You're a fucking asshole," the Rowdy blurted.

At that point, I had a choice. Cower or fight back. I chose to fight.

"*You're* a fucking asshole," I spat.

"Fuck you, piece of shit."

"Fuck *you*, piece of shit."

"You're a real bitch."

You're a real bitch.

"What did you call me?" the Rowdy said, scowling and steaming.

"A real *bitch*."

"Okay," the Rowdy said, turning the tables on the table-turning. "Here you go. Keep the change."

"Thanks for the tip," I said genuinely. "And thanks for coming in."

"Thank you too," he replied.

I felt like I was Sam the Sheepdog, and he was Ralph E. Coyote. Just punching the time clock after our conflict was over.

"Goodnight, Ralph."

"Goodnight, Sam."

I recently gave notice at the pub after getting a new job at the local GM dealership. At one point in the interview process, one of the accounting managers came in to talk with me.

"Hi, Brian," the manager said. "The sales manager really likes you, but I have some reservations about your resume."

"Okay," I said, not really surprised.

"Please explain to me how a pastor becomes a bartender."

"Well," I began, "I would say that I'm too progressive to work in the church. Church people would say that I'm too liberal to work in the church."

"Okay," the manager said, satisfied. "But why bartending?"

"I was going through some health issues and wanted to stay close to home. I applied at every place in town. Crofton has three second-hand stores, three coffee shops, and two pubs. So, I applied at them all. One of the pubs hired me."

"So, why car sales?"

"A friend who frequents the pub told me I'd be good at car sales," I explained. "Church work and pub work have taught me how to listen, how to assist, and how to sell. I've sold beer, and I've sold salvation. I can sell cars."

"The liquid product and the invisible product?" he said, smiling.

"Exactly," I replied, matching his grin.

"Well, you have my recommendation."

Tonight, my trainer at the dealership told me I need to be more upbeat. I'm too mellow.

"Is it okay that I tell you to be more upbeat?" he asked.

"Of course!" I responded, very upbeat. "You're suggesting that I need to still be myself but turn it up a notch."

"Exactly," the trainer said. "Be you, but more like a me-version of you."

Since starting work at the dealership, Lana tells me that I've become happier. Less mopey. I've definitely become friendlier. By contacting everyone I know to invite them to buy a vehicle from me, I've reconnected with people I haven't talked to in months—even years. Coming out of my cave and being outgoing is hard work but also rewarding. It reminds me of the time in Vancouver when I was going through a bout of depression and my doctor prescribed anti-depression meds. But at the last moment, she suggested that first I try exercising, eating healthy, and being more social.

It worked. I never used the meds.

I was listening to "Work" by Jars of Clay in my hot tub tonight.

> *I don't have a line of prospects that can give some kind of peace*
> *There is nothing left to cling to that can bring me sweet release*
> *I have no fear of drowning*
> *It's the breathing that's taking all this work*
> *Do you know what I mean when I say, I don't want to be alone?*

I don't really understand what that song is about. But I like it. Maybe it's about life. Life isn't work if you can just focus on the act of breathing. Compared to breathing, everything else should be easy.

I don't know what you find hard to do. Maybe loving your spouse. Maybe playing with your kids. Maybe dealing with assholes at work. Or talking to strangers about cars. Or being more upbeat.

It might be a good idea for us to stop thinking about our problems so much. And simply breathe in the spirit of God that is at work all around us. It's in your boss. It's in your enemy. It's even in your cat.

We've just gotta focus on the breathing.

Part Seven

THE MULTIVERSE

I will go, I will go

And march out from this grave

Through the low, from the low

I feel their feet dancing

You're alone, you're alone

You know how deep I sink

I'll let go, I'll let go

Just say that's what you need

The paralyzing truth —I am what I will choose

What am I if I'm done, waiting for you

—JIM ADKINS

WHY GOD MADE SUMMERTIME

Someone at the dealership where I work must love country music, because almost daily, I have the misfortune of hearing "Why God Made Summertime" by Blackjack Billy on XM Radio. (Did you know that you can have XM radio free for ninety days when you purchase a new car or truck from our dealership? Now that's something, right?)

> *Got the gang out back*
> *Sprinkler in the grass*
> *T-Bones grilling*
> *Cold Corona chilling*
> *Get your lazy on, all day long*
> *Let the sun shine*
> *That's why God made summertime.*

One morning as a young sales guy and I were filling balloons with helium, "Why God Made Summertime" was playing on the showroom radio station.

"I swear they play this song every morning," I said.

"What song?" Kid Salesman asked.

"Why God Made Summertime."

"God made summertime?"

"Yeah. It was one of his best creations."

"After boobs," he quipped.

"Beer was one of God's creations too. The monks made that."

"That's awesome," Kid Salesman replied.

"I guess that rounds out God's top three creations. Boobs, beer, and summertime," I summarized.

I've made four sales so far at my new job. A new Sonic LT Turbo, a lifted new Chevy Silverado diesel, a pre-owned Dodge Savana, and a pre-owned un-lifted Chevy Silverado. Some people tell me that I'm doing pretty good so far. I disagree. Kid Salesman told me that if I don't average twelve sales per month, I'm sucking ass. That's something I do not want to add to my growing list of life experiences. I want to do exactly what my sales manager suggests I do every morning: "Brian, today you're going to sell some fucking cars," he always says.

"I know I am," I always answer.

Car sales can be a cutthroat business. If you turn left instead of right or hesitate even for a second, a peer is ready to pounce. The other day I was walking toward a potential customer at the far end of the lot when, to my surprise, speeding past me in my left blind spot was a female sales consultant on a golf cart. She was going to intercept my customer.

"You're seriously racing out there to beat me to that customer?" I asked, incredulous.

"Yes, I am," Saleslady said unabashedly. "Sorry, sucka!"

"Unbelievable," I muttered.

She returned without a sale.

"You didn't miss anything," she said. "They were assholes who didn't want to talk."

"Yeah," I said, smiling politely. "They didn't want to talk to *you*. They may have talked with me."

This Saturday is my last shift at the pub. Thank God for that. It's figuratively killing me to work both jobs at the same time. The other night, I fell into a deep sleep, my butt on a barstool and my head on the laminate bar counter. I was so tired I just couldn't keep my slitted eyes open. It didn't help that there were no customers to keep me awake either.

When I finally woke up, I closed the pub early. I'm not normally allowed to do that, but I figured, what would be the worst thing that could happen to me: I'd get fired? That would be a blessing, not a punishment. I've been asking my boss to take me off the schedule for a while now, but she refuses. So, I finally put my sleepy foot down and quit. I agreed to finish the week, and then I would be gone.

As I was sitting in my hot tub after work, I looked north toward the mountains and noticed a lightning show taking place. Every minute or so, like there was some sort of storm schedule, there was a flash of light and a crack of electricity. It was amazing. My rational side kept telling me to get out of the hot tub, not because it could act as a lightning rod and kill me, like those unlucky new believers who once got electrocuted in a church baptismal tank, but because I needed sleep. But I couldn't leave. The lightning was too beautiful. I knew it was 1 a.m. and that I had to get up at 6 a.m. to work the next day at the dealership from 8 a.m. to 6 p.m. I knew I had to work after that at the pub from 7 p.m. to 1 a.m. I knew that the next day, I'd have to get up early and work at the dealership from 8 a.m. to 6 p.m. again and then back at the pub from 7 p.m. to 1 a.m. I knew it was in my best interest to get some sleep.

But the lightning was too beautiful.

The other day at the dealership, Kid Salesman asked me if I was really a former pastor. My nickname there is "Preacher."

"Yes," I replied. "I used to be a pastor. I still believe in God, and I still believe that Jesus was frickin' awesome."

"I'm not a religious person," Kid Salesman said.

"Neither am I," I said. "Neither was Jesus, for that matter."

"So, you're the type of believer who doesn't act crazy or believe that the entire Bible is true but still follows Jesus?"

"That pretty much sums me up."

"I can respect that," Kid Salesman said.

There's a verse in the Bible that says that every good and perfect thing in life is from God. It also says that God likes to give gifts to his kids. Like summertime, for example.

I've had a lot of good experiences this past year. I made a shit ton of friends at the pub, I discovered the therapeutic joy of writing, and I began a cancer protocol that is shrinking my brain tumor. And those are just three things off the top of my head. And if I pay attention, I know that each day going forward is going to be filled with good and perfect things as well.

But it will depend on me and the choices I make. Each day I have a choice to recognize the amazing things that God has put in my life or focus on the shitty things. Sure, occasionally, someone zips past me in a golf cart or makes me work too much, but when my eyes are set on the awesomeness, I quickly forget those sunspots.

Because the lightning is just too beautiful.

THE BIG SALE

I was in the pharmacy waiting for my foot fungus prescription the other day when I inadvertently told the truth. I'm a car salesman, and the stereotype is that we lie a lot.

I was sitting beside a woman in her early sixties who was also waiting for some medication. She shoulder-checked, noticed me, and asked me what I was selling. I was driven back. How did she know? What gave it away that I was a salesman? The wide tie? The white collared shirt? The weathered black slacks? Somehow this clairvoyant woman knew the truth about me. But I had her figured out, too. She had to be a mentalist.

"So, what are you selling?" Mentalist asked me.

"I sell cars and trucks at the GM dealership down the street. Are you in the market for a vehicle?"

"Ha-ha! I barely have enough money to buy food, let alone a vehicle," Mentalist said.

"That's shitty," I told her. "I'm sorry to hear that."

"It's okay," she said. "I get by. I heard there's a big sale on at your dealership."

At that point in our conversation, I was feeling sad for this woman. I was in a weakened emotional state. With my guard fully down, I blurted the truth.

"The big sale is bullshit."

At that point, everyone in the pharmacy laughed. I looked around, and all the eavesdroppers were smiling at me.

"Finally, a car salesman who tells the truth," one of the eavesdroppers proclaimed.

"What I meant is that the big five-day sale has been going on for nearly two weeks…" I whispered.

But no one was listening anymore. In their minds, I'd let the Chevy Silverado out of the truck corral. In their hearts, they felt vindicated. They now knew for certain that they had been duped when they bought their last car. The car salesman with the eighties tie and the bad case of athlete's foot had basically admitted it. It was as if I'd given them a signed confession of guilt. My tiny admission of wrongdoing was, to these people, an affidavit.

A tiny Punjabi woman came into the dealership the other day with a small piece of paper in her hand. It was a deposit slip. She was looking to get a refund for a deposit on a vehicle she never bought three months previous. So, I helped her obtain her money, and we began a friendship. Since that moment, she has purchased a little Chevy Spark from me, and I've purchased spicy butter chicken and vegetable samosas from her. Furthermore, I've helped her sell her curried wares to Credit Coach, Kid Salesman, and Lovely Receptionist. I'm hoping this will help her with the bi-weekly payments on her new Spark. But first I had to explain to her what a bi-weekly payment was.

"A bi-weekly payment is a payment that happens every two weeks instead of once a month or twice a month. As well, twice a year, instead of making the payment twice a month, you have to make it three times a month, because there are twenty-six bi-weekly payments in a twelve-month year. Make sense?" I asked.

"Yes. It sounds like white people's math," Punjabi Friend said.

"Yeah, I suppose it is. We encourage bi-weekly payments here, because it makes the payments look smaller to the buyer, helping us sell more cars. But to be honest, it really does help pay off the loan faster," I responded.

"So says the white person."

Want a surreal experience? Go have a meal at Smitty's in Duncan. You'll be surrounded by white and aboriginal senior citizens being served pancakes exclusively by Nepalese young men. How did I learn about this? Two Nepalese men came by the dealership inquiring about the new Chevy Cruze and our leasing rates. When they didn't come back the next day to finalize their vehicle purchase, I tracked them down at their place of work, Smitty's Nepalese Pancake House.

I had the Nepalese Nachos Supreme with Spicy Beef. When it came time to pay, the young Nepalese server gave me my bill and told me, with a huge smile, that he had given me a special discount. I thanked him and looked closely at my bill. There was indeed a discount. The Senior's Club discount.

I felt insulted and proud at the exact same time. I'm only forty-five. The server got a Denali-sized tip.

One of my favorite Bible heroes is a fellow named Jacob. He would have made a great car salesman. He knew how to lie and talk with word magic. He once traded for his brother's inheritance with a bowl of soup. He ripped off his uncle with enchanted goats. And he maneuvered himself out of a war with pissed-off relatives by wearing them down with row upon row of livestock, gifts, and servants. His name, Jacob, means "the Trickster."

Later in Jacob's story, he fights with an angel through the night till dawn, trying to make the "big sale." He loses, after being taken out at the ankles by the celestial wrestler, and learns an important lesson: God and his children do not exist to serve Jacob's needs, but Jacob exists to serve theirs.

A co-worker and I were recently trained by our boss to deliberately lie to people. We were instructed to call up people who were attempting to sell their used vehicles on autotrader. com and tell them that the dealership had a customer who wanted that exact car—and that we would pay cash for their vehicle. When the unsuspecting customer came in for an appointment, we would instead give them a low trade-in value on a new vehicle. We would appeal to their emotions as we tricked them through an elaborate bait-and-switch.

I couldn't do this tactic, but my young co-worker felt pressured to try. He told me later that at first it was difficult and that he felt guilty, but the more he lied, and the more money he made, the easier it became.

A few weeks ago, a young guy and his girlfriend came into my dealership office. He told me how he had been taken advantage of by a rival dealership. He overpaid for a Ram truck. As a result, his truck, which was now worth $25,000, had a debt owing on it of about $50,000. But there was nothing I could do to help him.

"They should teach young people in school how not to get ripped off by unethical salesmen," Young Customer said.

"I agree," I said. "I'm too new at this job to ever lie or rip off people for profit."

"You just wait," Young Customer said, "this place will change you, too."

Jesus once asked where the profit was if you gain the world but lose your soul.

At this point I'd like to explain to you why I exaggerate and invent the occasional detail in this book. I do so, because it makes for a more entertaining read. However, I always attempt to keep my stuff emotionally true. In my opinion, that isn't deceit; it's creative writing.

But the day I deliberately mislead a customer to make a profit is the day I quit the sales business.

I'd rather join my friends selling Nepalese pancakes at Smitty's and giving the Senior's Club discount to forty-five-year-olds.

That's an untruth I can stomach.

FOR A SECOND

There's a scene in the recent movie, *Ant-Man*, where the tiny costumed hero is battling the equally tiny supervillain, Yellowjacket, inside a briefcase that is falling out of an airplane. As they fall, Yellowjacket has an accidental conversation with the Siri app on his iPhone.

"I am going to disintegrate you!" Yellowjacket screamed at Ant-Man.

"Playing 'Disintegration' by the Cure," Siri said calmly to Yellowjacket.

At that point, "Plainsong," the first song on the *Disintegration* album, begins playing on the descending iPhone. It's a song about how even the worst sadness can have a hint of hope inside it.

> *I think it's dark and it looks like rain, you said,*
> *And the wind is blowing like it's the end of the world, you said,*
> *And it's so cold it's like the cold if you were dead,*
> *And then you smiled for a second.*

I like Ant-Man, because he's a messed-up guy who is given the opportunity to save the world, but more importantly, earn the admiration of his estranged daughter. He's thinking about others first.

When I was a kid, I used to pray every night that God would give me a super suit so I could fly around and help people. I truly believed God could give it to me. I believed he was personal and intervened in our lives to give us what he wanted us to have. I used to have the most vivid dreams of flying around in that super suit.

I don't believe God is personal like that anymore. At least not in my life. And I don't believe God will ever give me that super suit.

At work, I used to feel like a messed-up salesman. In one week alone, I lost three deals to the neighboring Ford dealership. Three deals. The customers took the rock-bottom offer I gave them over to Ford and leveraged my deals to get even lower prices. I think Ford was losing money on purpose just to make me feel small.

After the third lost sale, I texted Lana: *I feel so sad inside. I'm a shitty salesman. I just can't close deals. And the few sales I do get are all mini-commissions, because I get my customers such low prices.*

Lana: *You are too hard on yourself. Kick butt!!*

Me: *It's the other way around. My customers are getting sweet deals. But my ass is sure sore.*

A new salesman at work is really kicking butt. Not only is he making lots of volume sales, he's also getting large commissions from each deal—plus his bonuses and spiffs. I mentioned what a good salesman he was to the boss.

"That new guy was a great hire," I said.

"Yeah. But so were you," the boss replied.

"Thanks, boss."

One lesson they teach you in sales training is to mirror the customer. If the customer is upbeat, be upbeat. If the customer is laid back, be laid back. If they like hockey, so do you. If they're Buddhist, so are you.

Using this technique isn't new to me. One of my favorite Bible verses back in my professional evangelical days was by

Paul: "I become all things, to all people, in order to save some. To the Greeks, I'm a Greek. To the Jews, I'm a Jew."

I was selling a Chevrolet Sonic to a Tibetan customer the other day. This guy's name was pronounced something like "Ka-boom." He was a grinder. That means he worked the sales manager into practically giving the vehicle away. He ground us down to a no-profit deal.

While Ka-boom was in the finance office signing the papers for his practically free car, I was keeping his six-year-old daughter company. She's been in Canada for a mere six months. At one point in our visit, we saw the boss walk by.

"Who's that man with the fancy jacket?" Ka-boom's daughter asked.

"That's the boss. We all work for him," I explained.

"He's not the boss," the diminutive Tibetan said flatly.

"Yes, he is," I argued. "He owns this place. He's the boss."

Ka-boom's daughter disagreed again. "He's not the boss. The Dalai Lama is the boss."

"Oh. Right. And that means Jesus is the second boss," I suggested.

"No," she said, as forcibly as ever. "The Buddha is the second boss. Jesus is the third boss. And then it's the man with the fancy jacket."

A few days later, a new salesman was asking me and our new sales manager how much gas we put in the tanks of new car sales versus used car sales.

"So, if new car sales get a full tank of gas, what do used cars get?" the new guy asked.

"Nothing," the manager answered.

"He's joking," I said. "We give full tanks to all customers."

"At my last dealership, we only gave ten dollars to used-car purchases," the new guy said.

"At my last dealership, we siphoned the remaining fuel out of used-car purchases and sent the customers home with no gas at all," the manager said, straight-faced.

"Yeah," I said, attempting to join in the practical joke, "at my last dealership, the sales managers made the salesmen drink water all day long, so that when we sold a used vehicle, we could piss in the tanks…"

"—to at least make the needle move," the manager said, finishing my sentence.

I don't know what's in your tank these days. Maybe you feel like your gas has been siphoned out. Maybe you feel like the people around you are pissing in your tank. Maybe you feel like you've just got $10 in there. You'd give almost anything to just see the needle move.

I no longer believe I'm messed up. Want to know my secret?

I just keep busy. Ant-Man didn't beat Yellowjacket by sitting on his hands. He was always learning, always working, always trying. Ant-Man didn't sit around watching YouTube videos. He didn't think about how to entertain himself. Ant-Man kept moving.

I find that the less I think, the less sad I am. And the more I try to become helpful to those around me, the happier I am. I try to become all things to all people. Even today an indigenous customer told me that their white-people-eating dog probably won't gobble me up when I come over to deliver their used car on reserve land tomorrow.

He recognized how brown I was on the inside. And yes, their 2013 Dodge Avenger will have a full tank of gas.

So, if you see me and I look sad, just stare at me for a few more minutes. If you wait long enough, and if you can keep up with me, you'll eventually see me smile…even if it's only for a second.

TROUBLE ON CHRISTMAS EVE

It's Christmas Eve. Earlier today, I was at work selling cars. Well, no one was even looking at cars, let alone buying them. None of us were making sales calls either. Would you want a salesperson calling you on Christmas Eve?

So, I was just there waiting for the boss to send me home. I used the time to contemplate my life. And to write.

I'm feeling physically healthy again. It's been six months since I completed chemotherapy and radiation on my brain tumor. I've regained my weight, and I have plenty of energy. The only downside is that chemotherapy gave me a gift called peripheral neuropathy. That means the nerve endings all over the surface of my body are damaged. Toes tingle. Torso burns when touched. And legs prick with pins and needles after sitting. It's not a gift that's returnable. I may have to live with this indefinitely. But overall, not a high price to pay for a relatively clean bill of health.

My spiritual bill of health is not as clean. Never really was, I guess. Even earlier today, I was greedy. I'd tied for third place in the Ten-Day Pot of Gold contest with Saleslady. We were given a choice: split the $650 cash prize or settle the dispute with gross. That's when the sales managers add up the commissionable gross on her four deals and my four deals. The highest gross wins. What did I choose? I choose to go to gross. Why? I wanted to crush Saleslady and keep the entire $650 for myself.

Bad decision. Maybe I should have split the prize.

"Preacher," the sales manager said, laughing, "you lost by a landslide. Three of your deals lost money."

"Your average profit was only three hundred dollars per vehicle," the finance manager agreed. "We're thinking of letting you go, as you are costing us money."

"Congratulations, Saleslady," I said, feeling embarrassed. "Your commissionable gross was way higher than mine. You deserved the win."

"I'm outta here!" Saleslady shouted with a giant smile on her face and $650 in her hands. She drove the dealership golf cart directly to Walmart and bought Christmas presents for the staff members' kids, including mine.

Later, I texted Lana about it: *Saleslady just bought Trouble for our kids. The Despicable Me version with 17 Minion Movers. She was very happy.*

Lana: *Awe that makes me teary. How sweet. xoxo*

Me: *Yeah. I've started pretending that I lost to her on purpose.*

Bad decision? No. I'm glad I didn't split the prize. I didn't need the money. And my heart was wrong. I wanted to crush her. She wanted to give.

Apparently, that's the spirit of Christmas.

I watched *Star Wars: The Force Awakens* with my family the other day. Afterwards, Ellie had some questions.

"Why did Kylo Ren become bad?" Ellie asked.

"Everyone has a bad seed and a good seed inside," I explained. "We have to choose every day which seed we're going to water. Kylo Ren choose to water the bad seed."

"I choose to water the good seed," Ellie said, sweetly.

"Me too, dear," I responded.

I was in my hot tub last night listening to "I Will Go" by Jim Adkins.

I will go and march out from this grave...
The paralyzing truth—I am what I will choose.

At Christmas, we remember how God chose to come to Earth not to crush us but to save us from our bad seeds. We're meant to follow that example every day. God did not put me on Earth to crush people. I think he put me here to be kind to others.

At least that is what I learned today when Saleslady brought Trouble into my life.

MY RIDE

The other day I googled the following: "what the fuck should I do with my life?"

Selling cars and trucks fifty to seventy hours a week was no longer fulfilling for me. It's not that I wasn't good at it. I was great at it. I was the best-reviewed salesman at my dealership. I'd sold over a hundred vehicles in eleven months. I wasn't the top salesman, and I definitely was not the top grosser, but I was still making an honest living.

My secret? Give, give, give—but don't give away all the gross. Kids gotta eat.

It just wasn't fun anymore. It wasn't something to which I wanted to dedicate so much of my life.

I'd given up on many of the basics of the car-selling industry, such as cold calls. I'd also given up on trying to sell through social media. I told my boss I wasn't doing that shit anymore. Instead, I would become completely dependent on walk-in traffic and referrals. But you can't make a living that way. And by refusing to make cold calls, I was left with way too much time on my hands. When I have too much time on my hands, I start to think. And that's a bad thing. It reminds me of "Ride" by Twenty Øne Pilots.

I think about the end way too much.
I'm falling.
I've been thinking too much.

Help me.
So, I'm taking my time on my ride.

I remember one conversation I had with the boss a week before I quit.

"I heard you're looking for other work," the boss asked me.

"Yeah," I said, nervously. "Every six months, I have an MRI and get my head examined to find out if I have six months of health or six months of chemo. It's like having a six-month lease on life. Recently, I had a great brain scan, and I've realized that selling cars and trucks isn't what I want to do for the next six months."

"That's a terrible way to look at life. I believe that people are sick because they don't have a more positive attitude," the boss said sincerely.

"Well," I said, pausing at the simplicity of his last remark, "it's been great working here and I'll miss you.

Soon I found a new job. Or so I thought. I was hired at a hot tub dealership in Nanaimo, the same place I bought my hot tub spaceship.

But it didn't take long for that to grow old, too. I talked to Lana, and she told me to retire.

Now I'm forty-six and retired. Or you could say that I'm a stay-at-home dad. Or an out-of-work preacher.

You decide.

So, after I did my Google search, I stumbled upon a website that provided the guidance I needed: Kill your old life, find out what you want to do, and then do it.

What do I want to do? Preach about Jesus.

And when I'm not doing that? Take my time on my ride... and write.

HEATHENS

I signed my kids up for a community-center course on how
to be left alone at home. The program was aptly named Home
Alone. When they got back, I asked them about it. "How was
Home Alone?"

"It was okay," Hudson replied, passively.

"Did they teach you how to make traps?" I asked.

"Yeah," Hudson replied, getting more animated. "And when
criminals come to our house, what to do if your parents don't
believe you."

"Like dropping hot irons on crooks?"

"Yeah. Or buckets of paint."

The other day, Lana couldn't find her favorite jacket. She
figured it must have gotten misplaced during our move to
Nanaimo. More specifically, she thought that maybe Ellie and
I lost her leather treasure in our old place. So, early the next
morning, Ellie and I went to Crofton to look for it.

While we were searching the place from top to bottom, we
noticed that the deer that had been terrorizing my flowers had
fallen into the narrow ditch behind our house. Soon the local
fire department arrived and rescued the young buck while I
filmed the entire event. I posted the footage on Facebook, and
now more than fifteen million people have viewed the deer
rescue, many posting comments.

Viewer #1: *Everyone should watch and learn the meaning of
love and kindness.*

Viewer #2: *That's a stupid retaining wall.*

Viewer #3: *Gentlemen, your Karma points just went to a whole new level.*

Viewer #4: *Who puts up such stupid fencing???*

Viewer #5: *America could use more men like this.*

Viewer #6: *There's a place in heaven for you.*

Viewer #7: *I was scared when they decided to pull her up, it might scrape her tummy.*

Viewer #8: *I would have given the deer loads of kisses before I let him go.*

Viewer #9: *I held my breath the entire time.*

Viewer #10: *Beautiful lawn.*

My lawn *is* beautiful, because I paid someone a lot of money to make it beautiful. I'd been struggling with the lawn since I built this house. Bald spots, dead grass, rocks, and dandelions. I probably had the worst lawn on the block. So, I hired someone to haul away all the shitty topsoil I'd put there last year and replace it with top-grade stuff. Now I have the best lawn on the block. I'm glad that flower-munching stuck buck highlighted my victory for all to see.

Oh, and Lana's leather hoodie was buried under some luggage in her closet. In Nanaimo.

Am I criminal for having a dangerous ditch in my backyard? I never considered it. My kids played in there with no problems. I just wanted a lovely, level, lush lawn. I never meant to hurt any deer.

I've been listening to a lot of Twenty Øne Pilots lately. Their latest song is "Heathens."

> *All my friends are heathens, take it slow.*
> *Wait for them to ask you who you know.*
> *Please don't make any sudden moves.*
> *You don't know the half of the abuse.*

And now they're outside ready to bust,
It looks like you might be one of us.

I was chatting on the phone last night with a friend I met when I was twenty-one and he was twelve. We talked about our lives and shared pictures of our kids. His relationship with the law was always a bit dodgy.

"You still doing your pastor thing?" Dodgy asked me.

"Nope," I said. "Churches don't like me."

Dodgy laughed. "Why?"

"I'm not a good person, I guess," I said quietly.

"You're a great person! I'm not a good person. Trust me, I've been in my share of trouble," Dodgy replied.

"Oh, I trust you," I said. "I guess we're both heathens."

"If you're a heathen," Dodgy said, laughing harder, "then I'm a savage."

Jesus once said that it isn't what we do that defines us as good or bad but what comes out of our hearts. It's motivations that make us, not always actions.

If Lana hadn't gotten mad at me for losing her favorite hoodie, I wouldn't have gone to Crofton, and that poor deer would have died in my ditch. Sure, the jacket had been in her closet the entire time, but who cares? A deer's life was saved.

We're all heathens. We all need saving. And sometimes it's not the good people who save us...it's the heathens.

THE SPIRIT OF ADVENTURE

Since moving to Nanaimo, I frequently find myself thinking about when I was young. I grew up here and every place I go reminds me of my childhood. I can't stop from thinking about my growing-up experiences. For example, the other day my children and I walked past my old high school. We noticed a kid sitting alone at a picnic table.

I decided this would be a teachable moment: "What does Daddy tell you every morning before he drops you off for school?"

"Don't slam the truck door or you'll cancel Christmas?" the kids said timidly.

"No, the other thing."

"Take care of the lonely kids?"

"Right," I said. "Do you see that kid by himself over there at the picnic table?"

"Yeah," they replied.

"When your daddy went to that school, he would sit and eat lunch with that kind of kid."

"Really?"

"Yup. When I first went there, I tried to fit in with the popular kids, but it was far too stressful. So, instead I looked for other lonely kids to be friends with. It was so much easier. And much more fun."

At my father's funeral five years ago, someone I kind of remembered took me aside and shared a story about my dad with me. I'm not sure whether it was for my benefit or his. Probably mine.

"I'll never forget your father. When I was a small child, I regarded Mr. Pankratz to be an old guy. Eventually, I moved away, but years later returned for some kind of kids' program. I was really surprised to see Peter there at the front, dancing with the kids to a pre-recorded praise music video. As I considered this situation, I realized I was much older, in that moment, than your father was when I first thought of him as old. I remember there was a self-conscious smile on your father's face as he busted his moves to this cheesy but well-meaning music. Somehow, he seemed to be at once way out of his comfort zone and right in his element. In that moment, more than any other, I realized what kind of leader your father was. The kind I wanted to be."

That was about it. Basically, my dad didn't give a shit. If he could help, he would be there. Whether it was singing a solo in a church service, building a hip roof over the church portable building, leading the congregation to choose a new pastor, or disco dancing with kids in diapers—he didn't care. He was not living his life for the approval of others. Just for the approval of the One.

My father used to write when he was a young man: "I feel challenged to evaluate my own way of life. Have I drawn the line of differentiation between necessity and superfluity satisfactorily? Do I still have the energy at the end of a week to enjoy the finer things of life? It seems to me, if the spirit of adventure is not evident in my life, then I am too involved in the pursuit of material goods."

I'm nothing like my father. He never drank, never watched inappropriate movies, and never used power words. He went to church three times a week, if not four. Me? I drink, watch all kinds of movies, and occasionally swear like a motherfucker.

In fact, at this exact moment, I'm writing a blog with power words in it, drinking Rose wine mixed with ice and cranberry juice, and listening to a Twenty Øne Pilots rock song called "Screen" with its infamous 4/4 devil's beat.

> *While you're doing fine, there's some people and I*
> *Who have a really tough time getting through this life.*
> *So, excuse us while we sing to the sky.*
> *We're broken people, oh yeah.*

Yeah, I have started attending church regularly, and yeah, I have recently volunteered to help with a youth group my son is planning to attend in the fall. But that's not the same as Dad. His church commitment dwarfed mine.

But in terms of the spirit of adventure, we're the same. I guess we always have been.

TO HELL AND BACK

The other day I dusted off a journal of mine from 2003. As I read the ancient tome, one entry made me laugh. It was a description of my 5-year plan to grow church attendance from 80 to 380 members. The key to the plan? Everyone needed to invite friends. Why did I laugh when I read it? Because church people don't invite friends. That bit of information will help you understand why churches across Canada aren't growing; they're declining.

My analysis? The people who attend church don't believe what they think they believe. If they did, they would invite friends.

To be fair, some church people do believe what they think they believe, but these people also don't invite friends. Why? They know that church services are boring, awkward, and weird. Inviting friends to church would be counterproductive to helping their friends believe in Jesus. Church is weird. The Pope is weird. Speaking in tongues is weird. Trusting that a personal God is always watching me and has a plan for my life is weird. Believing that people go to hell is disturbingly weird.

I went to Neighborhood Ninja's birthday party the other evening. It was a Mexican-themed event. We played "Pin the Throwing Star on the Burro." We ate tacos shaped like shadows.

At one point, I disappeared from the melee and browsed the Neighborhood Ninja's private book collection. One sacred novel caught my eye: *Elminster in Hell*. It's a Dungeons and

Dragons novel. I learned that the immortal wizard, Elminster, once traveled through the seven levels of hell to close a breach opened by a horde of Shades. If Elminster failed to close the gap, the devils and demons would escape and destroy reality. With great effort, Elminster closed the portal but was consequently forced to remain there, forever, in hell. Luckily, he was soon rescued by his ex-girlfriend, Mystra, the goddess of all magic.

Weird.

Twenty-five years ago, I was attending a very conservative Bible college in Alberta. Outside the dean's office was a sign-out sheet for students planning to go away for weekends. We needed to inform the dean of our plans or face disciplinary action. One time, my buddy, Chairman Mao, decided to play a prank on the dean.

"Psst...Brian," Chairman Mao whispered. "Look what I did. Read the weekend sign-out sheet."

"It says your name and where you're planning to go. 'To hell and back,'" I whispered.

Chairman Mao giggled.

"So, you're going to hell and back for the weekend?" I asked. "Sweet! Can I come?"

I've spent most of my evangelical life trying to convince the Bible not to believe in hell. The idea that my friends who weren't Christians would be punished in eternal flames was abhorrent to me. It wasn't my friends' fault they didn't worship Jesus; it was the Church's fault. Church was just too weird.

After years of research, I eventually concluded that the Bible stands guilty as charged. It does teach the reality of hell for unbelievers. So, to preserve my spiritual integrity, I simply stopped believing in those parts of the Bible. Those verses offended God's spirit within me.

I resonate with the lyrics of "Unbelievers" by Vampire Weekend.

> We know the fire awaits unbelievers,
> All of the sinners the same.
> Girl, you and I will die unbelievers
> Bound to the tracks of the train.
> Is this the fate that half of the world has planned for me?
> But what holy water contains a little drop, little drop for me?

I feel awesome lately. My brain tumor is a distant memory. I'm working out and home-schooling my kids. I'm married to a foxy woman and retired at age forty-six. I'm praising the Lord, getting involved in a faith community, and making friends I can invite to church.

But I still think about the next life and wonder if there will even be one. What is my destiny? Heaven? Hell? Worm food?

I wouldn't be surprised if, when we die, every one of us is instantly uploaded to God's infinite computer hard drive. To live a life of virtual perpetual happiness. Heavenly Earth without the viruses. God's hard drive is probably located at the center of the moon.

Does that sound weird?

It makes more sense to me than any other weird theory I've heard.

Part Eight

THE VOYAGE HOME

All in all, nobody knows no one

Only one world is fast asleep

Can I find a way to let the last guard down

I'm opening the floodgates

I'm opening a window

I'm opening a doorway

I'm letting all the flies out

I've gotta torch my hideout

There's nothing left to find out now

While you're still away

Help out the ones who are falling

When they need no help at all

Always the ones who are calling

Sometimes it's nice to be called

—BIG WRECK

ParticipACTION

In the early 1970s, a piece of international news created a panic across Canada: the average sixty-year-old Swede was healthier than the average thirty-year-old Canadian. This news exposed Canadians as lazy and out of shape. Damn those Swedes for showing us up. In response, then-Prime Minister Pierre Trudeau jumped in, and the Government of Canada created the ParticipACTION program. It was designed to promote fitness and health among the chubbiest of Canadians.

One result of this initiative was that the Kinsmen Club, a local charitable organization in Nanaimo, bought forested land on Bowen Road and built the ParticiPARK. The Partici-PARK contained a fitness course consisting of twelve wooden stations hidden in the trees. These stations included fitness activities like push-ups, pole-climbing, and...wait for it... jumping.

I imagine that by now, few remember this bit of international news. And fewer still use the apparatus at the Partici-PARK. Push-ups in the trees? Jumping? I'm sure the Swedes felt really threatened.

Thirty-odd years ago, my church youth group played Capture the Flag at that park. The wooden apparatus was already old then. That was the first time I participated in a church youth group event. I remember that the volunteer leaders welcomed me and helped me have fun. Over time in that youth group, I learned how awesome Jesus was.

I've recently begun re-listening to the Christian bands I enjoyed thirty years ago. Bands like Steve Taylor, Daniel Amos, and the Choir. Did you know that all these bands are still creating new music?

I now volunteer as a church youth group leader in this town of my birth. The town where I first started following Jesus.

Which brings me to today's adventure. Hudson and I attended his first youth group function. I was his volunteer leader. We played Capture the Flag at the ParticiPARK on Bowen Road. The exact activity I did thirty-odd years ago, in 1983.

Alexander Pope once said: "Swift fly the years."

That average thirty-year-old Canadian from the news story? He is now seventy-six. That average sixty-year-old Swede? Dead.

Lately, I've been building Lego projects at night after the household has fallen asleep. Ahhh, Lego. I have a giant Rubbermaid tub of pieces collected from my children's many sets. Fifty-odd sets separated and dumped together unceremoniously. I have the original Lego-authorized booklets to help me rebuild these lost sets. Methodically. Accurately. Alone.

Lana says I'm riding some kind of crazy train. She's probably right.

Just prior to playing Capture the Flag, Hudson and I were eating blackberries by a fence near the ParticiPARK. I thought it would appear brave and heroic if I jumped over the fence to get at the best berries. So, I did. As I landed on the other side of the fence, I lost my balance and tumbled into a bramble of blackberry bushes on the edge of a steep embankment.

"Are you okay, Dad?" Hudson hollered into the abyss.

"Yeah. I'm fine. Just a few hundred scratches," I hollered back.

"And some big rips in your white shirt. I guess that's why they put a fence there."

"Yes, smartass. I guess that's why."

One of my favorite Bible verses is about living simple lives: "Make it your goal to live a quiet life, minding your own business and working with your hands."

I used to resent that verse. I'd look for other Bible verses to contradict it. Christians are supposed to be radical disciples, not quiet craftsmen. How can we save a lost world minding our own business?

Now that verse gives me hope. It's not up to me to save the world. I can relax and simply get involved in small charitable projects. Studies show that people who do so are happier.

When Ellie saw all my blackberry scratches, she almost cried. She's a sensitive girl. Or perhaps just a great actress.

"Oh, Daddy!" she cried. "Oh no. Oh no. Are you okay?"

"Yes, princess. I'm good."

"What happened to you?" Ellie asked.

"I got into a fight with a blackberry bush. I lost."

"Don't mess with my daddy, Blackberry Bush.

In 2047, this experience will be a thirty-year-old memory for Ellie and Hudson. Or completely forgotten.

As will everything we do, eventually. Whether we think we've accomplished something great or we just got involved in some small charity. It's all going to be forgotten someday. Should that truth keep us from getting involved in charitable activities?

The other day, I rode my bike to the Nanaimo River. It was like I was just there yesterday. But it's actually been thirty years. The names of past friends pop into my mind for random reasons. And as I look them up on Facebook, I realize I haven't talked to some of them in thirty years. Yesterday, I watched a video of Steve Taylor on the Internet. He looks leathered, wrinkled, and old. I found a mirror and looked at myself. I'm balding, grizzled, and old.

Part of me wants to die before I get really old. The other evening, my kids and I spent some time in my Crofton hot tub watching the Perseid meteor shower. My daughter was concerned that a meteor may land in our hot tub.

"Would we die, Daddy?" Ellie asked.

"I hope so," I blurted. "That would be the best way to die."

"Here lies our daddy, killed in his hot tub by a shooting star," Hudson said with aplomb.

While it's true that only a few people exercise at the ParticiPARK, what the Kinsmen accomplished way back when was not a wasted contribution. The ParticiPARK remains a beautiful forest in the middle of Nanaimo's urban sprawl. Animals play there, couples go for strolls there, and children have fun there. The ParticiPARK remains one of Nanaimo's greatest assets.

No effort to contribute is ever wasted. Even though it may be forgotten.

Thirty years ago, Steve Taylor recorded "Hero." I must have rewinded and replayed this song on my Sony Walkman cassette player countless times as a kid.

In a storybook land
I could dream what I read.
When it went to my head I'd see.
I wanna be a hero.
When the house fell asleep
From a Book I was led
To a Light that I never knew.
I wanna be your Hero.

So, here's my conclusion:

Jesus can be the Hero. And if there's a Devil, he can be the Loner. And I will be the happy guy who is quietly involved in a community doing meaningful stuff. Even if I get old and wrinkled. Even if my contributions seem insignificant.

And when that shooting star finds me in my hot tub, I hope it flattens me after a day of Capture the Flag in the ParticiPARK...not after a night of playing with Lego by myself.

LOVE IS ALL AROUND

I left the dealership eight months ago. Before I left, I inadvertently gave my phone number to a company that helps people get approved for car loans. When someone from that company contacted me recently, I told them I wasn't interested in their services. I guess they subsequently sold my phone number to the Nissan dealership here in Nanaimo, because this morning, as I was getting my family ready for church, I got a text from a fellow named Hank: *Are you looking for a car or truck?*

Part of me was irritated. It was 9 a.m. on a Sunday morning, and I was getting texted from a stranger who didn't care about me as a person but just wanted to sell me a car?

Another part of me felt love for Hank. Some random local car salesman was trying to support his family by showing the ambition to text a stranger at 9 a.m. on a Sunday morning. That shows commitment to the craft of auto sales.

I've recently changed my views on God. I now believe that God is everywhere. And since God is love, love is everywhere, just like air is everywhere. That means I can be controlled by the spirit of love anywhere and anytime I choose. Anyone can. And I no longer need to be controlled by anger, greed, or any other base emotion. Those base emotions were necessary when my ancestors were cave people desperate to survive, but I don't need them anymore.

Sometime after this theological discovery, Hudson said something that disrespected Lana.

"You shouldn't have been rude to your mother just now," I reprimanded Hudson.

"I wasn't," Hudson said, defiantly.

"I don't want to yell at you. I am no longer an angry person. Love is everywhere, and I can love you instead."

"Yeah, right," Hudson rebutted, "you want to yell at me."

"Part of me does," I agreed, "but I'm not a caveman anymore. I choose to love you. Give me a hug, and say sorry to your mother."

Hudson was stunned. "I'm sorry, Mommy," he said. "Please tell Daddy to stop hugging me."

It really worked for me. When I release my anger and fill that vacuum with God's love, I do and say things that may not have helped the caveman survive but which help my soul shine brighter.

I like to believe it's because of Jesus' life and death that we now have access to the energy of Love.

I quickly responded to Hank and he texted back: *Are you looking for a car or truck?*

Me: *Are you looking for salvation?*

Hank: *U applied online for a car loan and I got u approved!!*

Me: *Jesus loves you Hank.*

Hank: *Thanks Brian. I can get you financed for a vehicle:)*

Me: *I can get you a seat beside me in church this morning.*

Hank: *Ok that would be great! Then we can go for coffee and chat about your car loan.*

At that point, I figured it was time to let poor Hank off the hook. I bought a 2016 black GMC Sierra with a leveling kit, cold-air intake system, and cat-back exhaust system last March before I left the dealership.

Me: *I'm just fucking with you Hank. I bought a truck last March.*

Hank: *I'm glad you found a truck Brian. All the best.*

Me: *You too Hank.*

Mary Tyler Moore died recently at age eighty. As a kid, I used to watch her show and laugh with my family. It was a ground-breaking show for many reasons, including the fact it was written mostly by women.

Tributes poured in on Twitter with the hashtag #loveisallaround. I wondered what that meant. So, I searched online and discovered the lyrics of the theme song for the *Mary Tyler Moore Show*.

> *Love is all around, no need to waste it*
> *You can have a town, why don't you take it*
> *You're going to make it after all.*

Was it a coincidence that I learned this news the same day that I told my kids about the overwhelming pervasiveness of love? I didn't used to believe in coincidences. I still don't. But now that I've realized that love, like gravity, is all around me, I am no longer surprised when love happens to me. Why shouldn't love guide me? It's everywhere. The universe is conspiring to connect people to the spirit of love all the time.

I was editing the chapter of this book entitled "Free Bird" the other day. That same day, as I was talking with Ellie about life at school and the importance of not allowing others to define who we are, Hudson joined the conversation.

"Only you can define you, Ellie," I said. "If anyone doesn't like the fact you wear the same shirt every day, then they can just step off. You are free."

"Free bird," Hudson said, almost to himself.

"What did you say?" I asked excitedly. "Were you reading my book? Have you been listening to Lynyrd Skynyrd?"

"No," Hudson said. "I just felt like saying that."

"Weird," I said, in awe of this little mystery.

But it isn't weird. And it's not a mystery. Love is all around, scripting events for the loving benefit of the dreamers, the lovers, the artists, and the compassionate. It's the spiritual law that is opposite to the second law of thermodynamics.

Second Law of Thermodynamics: There is a natural tendency of any isolated system to degenerate into a more disordered state.

Life sucks.

First Law of Love: All things can work together for the purposes of love if you want them to.

Love rules.

After I said goodbye to Hank, we headed to church. But as we arrived at our destination, we discovered church had been cancelled due to snow.

"Yay! Now we can go home!" the kids cheered.

"Yeah, no," I said, popping their bubble. "Now we're going on an adventure. We'll find another church. We have a truck, and Love will guide us."

"Aw, Dad," Hudson whined, "let's go home."

"When life gives you lemons, allow the universe to show you the lemonade," I said.

"What does that mean?" Ellie asked.

"It means that when things don't go the way you want in life, be patient, and you will find something better. Sometimes the good is the enemy of the best. Going home would be good, but finding another church to attend may be the best."

"I understand, Daddy," Ellie said, putting it all together. "Hudson is my lemon."

Since moving to Nanaimo last June, I don't see Neighborhood Ninja much anymore. So, Lana and I recently invited him to Nanaimo to have supper with us at the Keg. During our visit, we discussed life, God, and my theories on love.

"God is everywhere," I said, hoping for a lengthy conversation.

But Neighborhood Ninja would have none of it. "I vowed a long time ago not to try and understand God, because it's too complicated."

"You went to university at age fifteen, because you're an idiot savant. You understand complicated economic, political, and historical theories. Plus, you're a freaking ninja who just passed the triple black belt exam in Japan with a broken arm," I exclaimed.

"All true," Neighborhood Ninja said. "But religion is just too complicated."

"God is everywhere," I said again, under my breath. "And since God is love, love is everywhere. How is love complicated?"

I haven't written anything in a long time. Life just got busy. But recently, a close friend I call Big D encouraged me to start writing again. While I was sitting in the boring church that the spirit of love guided us to this morning, I shot Big D a text: *Our church was cancelled today. So, we went to a different one. I'm sitting here right now being bored to tears.*

Big D: *I decided to be bored at home this morning.*

Me: *Studying?*

Big D: *Yeah. It felt like a better choice than listening to a cliché homily about self-congratulating, culturally contextualized morals.*

Me: *That's what I'm listening to right now.*

Big D: *I miss Hot Tub Spaceship pastor.*

The conclusion of the matter?

Yes, the lemonade church was sentimental and boring, and the sermon I barely listened to was self-congratulating and full of culturally contextualized morals. But afterwards, I met a guy whose son is in Hudson's class at school. He, like me, is a disillusioned former church planter. Cool, right? Maybe. Maybe not. Time will tell. But even if this new relationship goes nowhere, I still got to reconnect with Big D and I subsequently wrote this new episode.

God is everywhere. And since God is love, love is everywhere. I don't want to waste it.

Oh, and if you're looking to get pre-approved for a car loan, Hank is your man.

MY SECRET TO A HAPPY LIFE

I sometimes wonder if I'm happy or not. How can I tell? Sometimes I just feel sad. I know that spending money doesn't help. That kind of happiness is fleeting. That's why I don't like going to shopping malls. Music helps. I went to the Switchfoot concert in Vancouver with some friends last week. For most of the concert, I felt happy. But when we left, it was so cold and blustery outside that much of my happiness was swept away. I became determined to explore this thing called happiness and try to figure it out. Here are my observations on the matter.

Yesterday, I was shoveling snow off the sidewalk in front of my house in Nanaimo, and a visibly happy woman walked briskly past me and said, "Isn't it great when you enjoy what you're doing?"

She must have been projecting her own feelings of brisk walking joy, because I wasn't feeling it. I could think of many things I'd rather do than shovel snow. I'd been shoveling snow every other hour during the snowstorm. Sometimes I wish I wasn't so OCD that I need to have the nicest sidewalk on the block.

"Should I stop if I'm not enjoying what I'm doing?" I asked before she walked too far. She laughed awkwardly, picking up her pace.

"Do you enjoy the snow-swept sidewalk?" I said, loud enough for her to still hear.

She turned her head slightly. "Well, I do appreciate it."

"Then I'm glad!" I said happily.

And off she briskly went.

Lana and I recently sold our Vancouver home. We used the profits to pay off debt. I told Big D about our situation.

"Paying off that debt must have made you happy," Big D said.

"I don't know if I felt happy," I replied.

"What did you feel?"

"I felt the absence of stress. Is not having a feeling a feeling?"

"I guess so," Big D replied. "All I know is that I'm happy for you."

I'm currently employed as a part-time janitor. My co-worker is named Janet. I call her Janet-tor.

I work four hours a night cleaning the Fortis and Shaw buildings in Nanaimo. My Shaw boss is very particular. Almost daily, he texts me pictures of garbage containers that have a smudge or a loose bag. He even gave me a map of the entire Shaw building with a six-color-coded scheme to show me the locations of the large garbage, small garbage, paper recycling, mixed recycling, organics, and hard plastic recycling containers. There are over a hundred colorful dots on this map. It's like a Georges Seurat painting. He often asks me to do a better job.

"It will be my pleasure," I always tell him.

Am I lying? Because, in reality, I find my boss annoying. To be perfectly honest, I laugh at him for taking so many pictures of garbage containers. He must be more OCD than me.

One of my favorite Bible verses is something from James: "Consider it pure joy when you face hard times. If you hang in there you will get personal maturity."

According to James, Jesus' half-brother (same mother, different father), if you're not happy right now, you might be later. And if you're not, at least you'll be mature.

Cold comfort.

I was listening to a show on CBC about a rabbi who was expelled from his religious community for no longer believing as they did. He lost everything dear to him, including all contact with his children. This fellow, Shulem Deen, described how he subsequently found a happiness he wouldn't have had if he had silenced his doubts and stayed on as an unbelieving believer. His happiness? He discovered the joys of writing and free thinking.

The biblical word for "mature" refers to the idea of being complete, not lacking anything.

I'm told there's a Buddhist expression that says awareness is suffering.

I often used that expression with my customers when I was a car salesman. Car shoppers would come in with a particular budget, and I'd show them a vehicle that met their budget. Invariably, they would ask about different vehicles with more features. I knew that if I showed them the nicer vehicle, they would either go home with a vehicle they originally said they couldn't afford or the affordable vehicle they didn't love anymore, because it was missing the fancier features.

The awareness of enhanced features is suffering.

Switchfoot sang "If the House Burns Down Tonight" at their concert.

> *Put your hand in mine and*
> *Put your heart in drive.*
> *We got everything we need yeah*
> *Left it all behind us.*
> *What we need will find us.*

The idea is that if our homes and everything we've bought burn to the ground, we can still be happy. If we're aware, we will always have what we need.

As I've been thinking about what makes me happy, I realize I haven't been aware of the obvious. It's not money or approval from my boss or the satisfaction one gets from shoveling snow. It's the laughter I find in these events. The joking with Big D, the absurdity of my boss, the playful banter with brisk strangers on the street. Humor makes me happy.

I guess awareness doesn't always have to bring suffering either.

Tonight, Lana and I took our kids to the Keg and then to a play called *Oliver Twist*. We want to make the kind of family memories that survive house fires. Things didn't go according to plan though. The kids were squabbling and making our lives unhappy. Hudson was being particularly mean and surly. So, Lana took Ellie to park the car, while Hudson and I went into the restaurant to secure a table. He entered first, and I decided to play a trick on my unhappy son. I turned around, left the restaurant, and hid in the bushes outside. He was alone in the lobby. When he came out to find me, I jumped out and scared him.

"Where'd you go?" Hudson asked.

"I wanted to burn you," I said. Hudson laughed.

"You should apologize now," I added.

"For what?" he asked.

"For being an asshole before," I reminded him. He laughed harder and headed toward his approaching mother to apologize.

As we shared that big laugh, I was aware of how happy I was.

As Lana arrived, she noticed the improvement in Hudson's attitude. But we weren't out of the woods yet. Ellie was very upset about the lack of gluten-free items on the menu.

"I told you our kids didn't deserve the Keg," I said to Lana, half-joking.

"You're right," she replied, with a wink. "I thought our kids were better than they are."

I laughed. "That's hilarious!"

Again, I was happy. Laughter was what I needed. And laughter had found me.

This is going to be a happy life after all.

BULLET THROUGH THE GRAVE

I've been thinking about death again. Not the act of dying or when I'll die but what to do with my body after the Grim Reaper takes my soul. Cremation maybe. I googled what to do with cremated remains and found one website that had twenty-seven suggestions. Twenty-seven? That's a shit ton of options. Some of the weirder ones were putting the ashes into a pencil set, into tattoo ink, and even into a bullet. I asked my kids what they preferred.

"If I get cremated what should we do with the ashes?"

"Definitely a bullet," Hudson said immediately.

Ellie hesitated a second, and then said, "So, if you die from a gunshot, I can shoot them back—with you!"

We no longer call Ellie short, like we used to. Insults of any kind make her angry. Now Hudson calls her fun-sized.

Cremation isn't my first choice. Or even my second. We went to the Nanaimo Home Show the other day. A funeral guy was there with a booth. I asked him how much it would cost to have my body buried close to my father in the Chinese graveyard near where I grew up. He said it would be about $5,000. I used to walk past this graveyard every day for three years on the way to junior high. I would dream about making a samurai movie in it. With cowboys.

My first choice, until recently, was cryogenic freezing. This is a procedure where your body, or just your head, if you're on a tight budget, is frozen until a treatment is invented that will revive you in the future and cure your illnesses, which are presently incurable. Like what happened to Captain America. The company is called Alcor, and they're based in Scottsdale, Arizona. That's also where the Arizona Cowboy College is located.

I was drawn to this option, because I don't think heaven is real. At least not in the way it's commonly taught in church. So, wouldn't getting my body frozen until I can be cured of cancer be a good back-up plan?

Then I found out that the cost for the whole body is US$200,000. The procedure for just a head is US$35,000. In contrast, Cowboy College is only US$2,250 for the entire week.

I still considered the frozen head option though. There's a great sketch from the *Mighty Boosh* where Howard Moon and Vince Noir also consider it.

"Well, I'm going to have my head frozen cryogenically, okay?" Howard says to Vince. "And then I'm going to be put in a jar and then twelve thousand years from now, they'll revivify me, and I'll be the head...in a jar...and they'll wheel me out at ceremonies and consult me like an oracle. It'll be great."

Vince replies, "Why don't you just get your whole body frozen?"

"That's not the way it works in the future, Vince," Howard says, sighing. "It's just heads, floating about, consulting each other at ceremonies."

"Really," Vince says sarcastically.

I've been feeling very proud of my family lately. Lana has achieved her dream of becoming a successful and sought-after family mediator. Ellie has overcome many personal challenges to be near the top of her class in English and math (and still find time to help write and co-star in a musical at her school about modern-day slavery). And Hudson has come out of his shell to become a very encouraging and popular friend to everyone in his class. His teacher and I had a conversation yesterday about his progress.

"So, how's he doing?" I asked.

"He's starting to put his hand up in class which is awesome," the young teacher said, bubbling.

"Oh good," I replied.

"And today he gave his speech to the class that was fantastic," she said excitedly. "It was pretty short though."

"You mean fun-sized," I corrected.

My son's fun-sized speech, or devotion. as they call it in Christian schools, was based on 1 John 3. The topic of the devotion was love: "This is the message which you heard right from the start...that we should love one another."

In a sense, my feelings of pride in my family come from the same part of me that wants to live forever. Albert Einstein once said something about our families and the future: "Death is not an end because we can live on in our children...for they are us."

When I see my wife and children doing things and becoming people I've always hoped for them, it's almost like looking into the future. They have wonderful lives ahead of them, and it's humbling to be able to see it so early.

Later in his letter, John writes about the connection between love and immortality: "God is love; those who rest in love rest in God, and God rests in them...so we may have confidence after we die."

In other words, there *is* a life coming after we die. And in that life, we will rest in God's love.

Instead of worrying about the afterlife or making plans to have my fun-sized head cryogenically preserved for a career as a ceremonial consultant, I can just chill.

So, what will I do with my body after I die? I'm going to pay that $5,000 and be buried in the Chinese graveyard with my father. I don't want my kids drawing sketches of me with my penciled ashes. Or seeking revenge on criminals with bullets filled with me. And being cryogenically frozen and revivified one hundred years from now is a vain pursuit and a lame back-up plan. It's not motivated by love but by fear and restlessness. Besides, with the money I save by not being frozen, I can finally go to Cowboy College.

I'm still not sure if heaven is real. But I like the idea of my soul floating around forever in a jar of God's love.

FLOODGATES

When we moved to Nanaimo, sold our Vancouver home, and got out of debt last year, Lana told me I could purchase any two things I wanted. I knew immediately what I would get. An electric longboard and…wait for it…a hot tub.

My electric longboard arrived last month, and my new hot tub was installed last week. So, what does a typical day hold for this semi-retired stay-at-home dad, skateboarding out-of-work preacher, and late-night janitor? I wake up, jump in the hot tub, get the kids to school, clean house, skateboard to the library and back, prepare and eat a healthy supper with my family, go to work, come home, jump back in the hot tub with a red Solo cup full of red wine from Rainy Crick mixed with cranberry juice while listening to the new Big Wreck album and then jump out of the hot tub to watch a movie. Then I write.

As you can see, I'm neither super-stressed nor super-motivated these days.

Unlike my boss when I was a car salesman. He was hyper-driven. He intimidated me. I'd do my best to avoid him and his intensity. The worst was when he got involved in deals I was making with customers. One time I was attempting to sell a Chevy Malibu to a single woman expecting a baby. She was concerned that her infant car seat wouldn't fit comfortably into the back of the new car. It didn't. Then my boss got involved.

"I don't think there's enough room back there," the expectant mother said, screwing up her face, like she was trying to do the math.

"There absolutely is," the boss said. "Brian is our infant car seat expert at the dealership. He's been trained specifically in this area. He'll show you."

"Is that true?" she asked me.

"Um…" I murmured.

"He's the best," the boss said, continuing the deception.

Later the boss left the room to see if he could crunch the numbers more in her favor. Salesmen love saying they're going to crunch numbers. Generally, it means that they're going to reconsider how much profit they can live with. It's always about profit. While he was gone, the woman and I talked.

"What should I do?" she asked.

"I think you should stay with your current vehicle and save up more money to get a mini-van," I said, honestly.

"Are you talking me out of this? You're a terrible salesman," she said, not joking.

"Thank you." I smiled back.

The boss re-entered the room and closed the deal. In a few weeks, the woman and her baby returned demanding a refund for being misled.

I don't feel bad that I am not a profit-driven person like my former boss. I've come to realize that I'm driven in other ways. For example, I'm always thinking about God and church. On top of that, I'm curious about the little miracles that happen all around us every day.

Carl Jung once said something about life: "The privilege of a lifetime is to become who you truly are."

I know who I am. And I've summarized it thusly.

My Twitter profile: *Bold not a bully Imaginative not heretical Emotional not sentimental Driven not hasty Damaged not broken Insecure not in despair In Christ not Christianity.*

When I was in Bible college (a place Christian nerds go to feel popular), my friend, Chairman Mao had a nickname for me: The Wind.

"Brian, you're like the wind," Chairman Mao said. "Your opinions and beliefs keep changing without notice."

"What do you mean?" I asked.

"Almost every other day, you come into my dorm room to explain something you've figured out about life. You change your opinions like the wind changes directions."

I prefer the term "evolving." As I'm blown about by the winds of new information, I *must* keep changing my beliefs. I'm good with that. I feel sorry for people who still believe the same things they believed in childhood. To be alive is to evolve.

I was in my new hot tub this evening listening to a Big Wreck song, "Floodgates."

> *Oh, reach out to those where the shine is*
> *As they refuse to be found.*
> *Can I find a way to let the last guard down?*
> *I'm opening the floodgates.*

The idea to me is that I can learn from those who are also curious about life. Their ideas are deep and challenging. As I think and learn and eventually share, I also am opening the floodgates.

Who are you? Are you evolving, or are you the same person you were a year ago? Do you have the same beliefs you had when you were a teenager? That would be a shame. And if you are growing, are you sharing those changes with people you care about? I hope so. I don't want to be the only one.

MY BUTTER

Today is April 2, 2017. I began this writing adventure almost three years ago to sort out my beliefs and to create a memoir for my kids to read after I'm gone.

During these past three years, I've owned two hot tubs, lived in three homes, held five jobs, undergone seven MRI scans, and written sixty-three chapters of this memoir.

At this moment, it's 28°C, and I'm sitting under the board-walk at Clearwater Beach, Florida, watching my family play together on the white sands of the Gulf of Mexico. We're here on vacation to build family memories at the Disney theme parks and other points of interest in and around Orlando.

Yesterday, I tried in vain to persuade my daughter to play shuffleboard with me at the resort.

"Let's play shuffleboard together," I pleaded.

"No, Daddy," Ellie said. "We can just watch the shuffleboard channel on TV together."

There is no shuffleboard channel on TV.

But now it's the kids who are being active in the ocean while I sit and type these words into my phone screen. It's nice to see my children having fun together. Like most kids, they squabble occasionally. I try to teach them to listen to the voice of God that's inside us and not get offended by each other so easily.

In an interview on CBC radio the other day, Jean Vanier said that we all have the voice of God inside us: "Different people call it different names—conscience, spirit, love, knowledge of right and wrong. The trick though is discipline. Part of discipline is community. Community is a sign that love is possible in a materialistic world."

During our first day at materialistic Disneyworld, my little community of four lost our rental car for over an hour in the parking lot as we tried to leave the happiest place on earth. I guess I didn't pay close enough attention to where I parked. The following day, Lana decided she would park the car at the Magic Kingdom instead of me. Then she insisted that we all memorize where we parked.

"Okay, everyone," she said, "where did Mommy park?"

"Unicorn Section, Row P," the kids replied.

"Mommy parked in Unicorn P," I reiterated, with a smirk.

"Hee-hee. Unicorn pee." Ellie laughed quietly.

It's hard not to be upset sometimes by quarreling siblings, maze-like parking lots, and media-swamped children. Most people think the solution to this frustration is to be more patient, act kinder, or make an attitude adjustment.

They're wrong.

The pastor of the church we attended in Orlando put it best: "The better solution is heart transformation, not behavior modification."

There are two ways to be a better person—work harder at it, or think about God's love more. The latter takes discipline.

Hudson and I love butter. He was even dipping his steak into butter the other day. Ellie didn't find that acceptable. "That's disgusting," she said.

"No, it's good," Hudson said. "Everything goes better with butter."

"Does ice go better with butter?" Ellie rebutted. I could smell a fight coming on.

"Well..." Hudson began.

"Stop squabbling," I said quickly. "Everything *does* go better with butter. End of discussion."

Ellie didn't miss a beat.

"Then Hudson is my butter," she said sweetly.

I guess love is possible in a materialistic world after all.

AFTERWORD

Not long ago I was enjoying coffee on an outdoor patio downtown with a friend, when we were suddenly distracted by loud, agitated yelling from down the street. A glance revealed a disheveled homeless man, aggressively screaming unintelligibly at passersby. As we watched, he stalked down the sidewalk and turned his verbal onslaught towards a tall, lithe, blonde man carrying a skateboard and began curdling the summer air with a string of imaginative profanity.

As we watched this little street drama unfold, my heart suddenly double-skipped as I recognized the man in his path as my friend, Brian.

I quickly got up, told my coffee buddy to sit tight, and began running down the road, adrenaline pumping, towards what I thought was an impending assault. But as I got closer, I saw something that slowed my jog to a walk: the look on Brian's face. It was perfectly calm, revealing his tireless, disarming smile. He was cheerfully chatting to the guy like he does to everyone who crosses his path. Before I could get closer, the homeless fellow suddenly nodded, became quiet, turned, and walked away.

It wasn't until later that I asked Brian what that had been all about. "Oh," he said, "just making friends."

For me, that response reveals the essence of the person Brian has chosen to become through the greatest struggles of his life.

Many times over the years I have walked alongside struggling people who have experienced tremendous loss: Unexpected illness, shattered relationships, aborted careers. The resulting spiritual crisis is often fraught with resentment, self-pity, guilt, and shame.

Yet, every now and then, if we are fortunate enough, we meet someone who has suffered great loss and somehow comes through it with unusual serenity and a magnanimous self-assurance that takes us off guard. Which is what happened when I first met Brian and heard his remarkable story.

His relentlessly honest embrace of the crap reality of circumstances beyond his control has been met with an equally relentless passion for life, fueled by his curious love for some guy from ancient Palestine they called Jesus. The result? An inspiring, headlong, unorthodox, and faith-affirming trip that has opened my own hot tub-fogged eyes to stars in the night sky that I had never noticed before.

Steve Jobs, in his famous commencement speech, said that, "death is the destination we all share. No one has ever escaped it... It is life's change agent." As he would put it later in the speech, "Your time is limited, so don't waste it living someone else's life. Don't be trapped by dogma - which is living with the results of other people's thinking. Don't let the noise of others' opinions drown out your own inner voice. And most important, have the courage to follow your heart and intuition."

Perhaps that is an experience reserved only for those rarest of adventurous, open souls.

I like to think you have just joined me in the privilege of meeting one of them through these pages.

—Rod Kolke, Pastor.

ACKNOWLEDGEMENTS

My thanks go out to the people who made this book possible. First and foremost are those who have been reading my blogs over the past four years. If it wasn't for your constant encouragement, I would have quit writing a long time ago.

Special thanks must go to my good friend, Troy, for not only writing the foreword to this book but also for providing the comprehensive first edit. His kind thoughts on the book went a long way to getting me to the point where I'm actually getting this thing published.

For being so generous with their time, special thanks to Zoe and Kevin and everyone else at FriesenPress. Thanks for walking me through this self-publishing process, and especially for the second (and third) exhaustive copyedit. Kevin's encouragement to move forward became a key waypoint along the journey.

Rod, thanks for your friendship and support, and for writing the afterword.

And, of course, to my family: Lana, Hudson, and Ellie. It would be a pretty thin book without you guys in my life.

—Brian Pankratz
www.hottubspaceship.com

Hot Tub Spaceship: Volume Two *is coming soon!*

PRAISE FOR HOT TUB SPACESHIP

Vancouver: *I really enjoy your writing. You still inspire and challenge my faith. Thanks for doing that!*

Ottawa: *Your stuff just keeps getting better and better. I am faster to click the link with each entry.*

Tofino: *I love reading your words…it takes me back and keeps me tied to Jesus in the same way I was drawn to him.*

Victoria: *Love your writing and I think maybe you should write a book.*

Burnaby: *Funny!*

Vancouver: *Pretty sick lookin book you got here. I think I'll catch it.*

Courtney: *I read your stuff and enjoy the weaving together of stories and thoughts.*

Princeton: *Oh, but how I so LOVE reading what you write. You really have no idea.*

Calgary: *So much heart and authenticity…It's really amazing to see how much you're willing to share from your raw experiences.*

Edmonton: *You always makes me smile. I love reading your raw, honest words.*

White Rock: *Keep up the writing...I always look forward to reading it.*

Crofton: *You make me laugh every time. I love reading your stuff it makes my day*

Fort Langley: *Love it. Thank you. Needed to hear it.*

Mission: *You word-weaver you. It's like you knitted a ninja outfit with words.*

Duncan: *It is sooo refreshing to see someone so open. Thank you for pouring out your heart. It really inspired me today.*

Westholme: *You should really think about taking up writing as a career. You have a real talent.*

Toronto: *Thanks for sending me that. It was really good.*